The Complete Guide To Becoming A Shoestring Millionaire

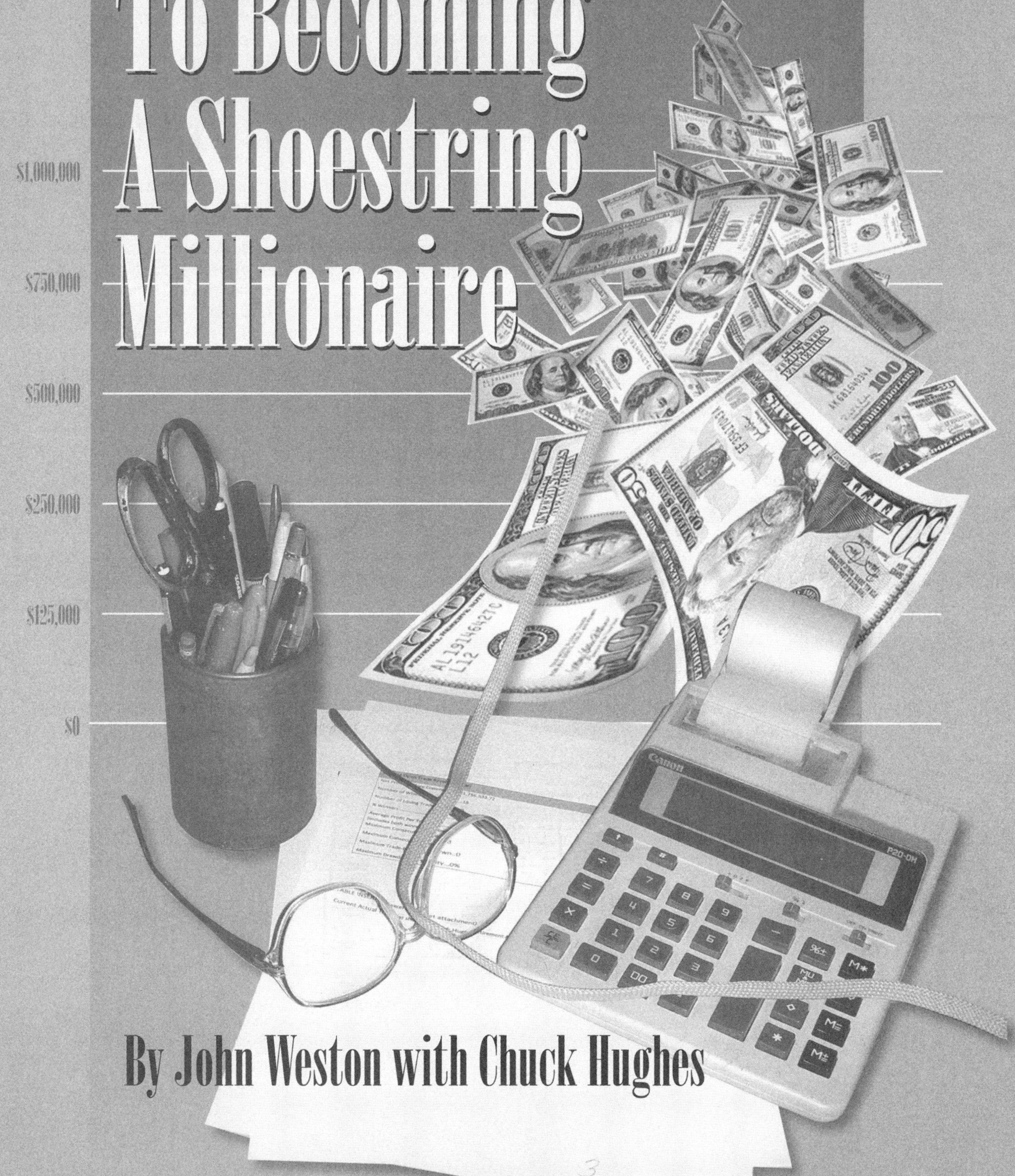

By John Weston with Chuck Hughes

Information within this publication contains "forward looking statements" within the meaning of Section 27A of the Securities Act of 1933 and Section 21B of the Securities Exchange Act of 1934. Any statements that express or involve discussions with respect to predictions, goals, expectations, beliefs, plans, projections, objectives, assumptions or future events or performance are not statements of historical fact and may be "forward looking statements." Forward looking statements are based on expectations, estimates and projections at the time the statements are made that involve a number of risks and uncertainties which could cause actual results or events to differ materially from those presently anticipated. Investing involves the risk of loss as well as the possibility of profit. All investments involve risk, and all investment decisions of an individual remain the responsibility of that individual. Option and stock investing involves risk and is not suitable for all investors. Past performance does not guarantee future results. No statement in this book should be construed as a recommendation to buy or sell a security. The author and publisher of this book cannot guarantee that the strategies outlined in this book will be profitable and will not be held liable for any possible trading losses related to these strategies.

All information provided within this publication pertaining to investing, options, stocks and securities is educational information and not investment advice. Legacy Publishing is not an investment advisor and recommends all readers and subscribers to seek advice from a registered professional securities representative before deciding to invest in stocks and options featured within this publication. None of the material within this publication shall be construed as any kind of investment advice. Readers of this publication are cautioned not to place undue reliance on forward-looking statements, which are based on certain assumptions and expectations involving various risks and uncertainties that could cause results to differ materially from those set forth in the forward looking statements. Please be advised that nothing within this publication shall constitute a solicitation or an invitation to buy or sell any security mentioned herein. The author of this publication is neither a registered investment advisor nor affiliated with any broker or dealer.

Although every precaution has been taken in the preparation of this publication, the publisher and author assume no liability for errors and omissions. This publication is published without warranty of any kind, either expressed or implied. Furthermore, neither the author nor the publisher shall be liable for any damages, either directly or indirectly arising from the use or misuse of the book. Users of this publication agree to indemnify, release and hold harmless Legacy Publishing, its members, employees, agents, representatives, affiliates, subsidiaries, successors and assigns (collectively, "The Companies") from and against any and all claims, liabilities, losses, causes of actions, costs, lost profits, lost opportunities, indirect, special, incident, consequential, punitive, or any other damages whatsoever and expenses (including, without limitation, court costs and attorneys' fees) ("Losses") asserted against, resulting from, imposed upon or incurred by any of The Companies as a result of, or arising out of this agreement and/or your use of this publication. This publication is designed to provide accurate and authoritative information in regard to the subject matter covered. It is sold with the understanding that the author and publisher are not engaged in rendering legal, accounting, or other professional services. If legal advice or other expert assistance is required, the services of a competent professional person should be sought. Use of the material within this publication constitutes your acceptance of these terms.

HYPOTHETICAL PERFORMANCE RESULTS HAVE MANY INHERENT LIMITATIONS, SOME OF WHICH ARE DESCRIBED BELOW. NO REPRESENTATION IS BEING MADE THAT ANY ACCOUNT WILL OR IS LIKELY TO ACHIEVE PROFITS OR LOSSES SIMILAR TO THOSE SHOWN. IN FACT, THERE ARE FREQUENTLY SHARP DIFFERENCES BETWEEN HYPOTHETICAL PERFORMANCE RESULTS AND THE ACTUAL RESULTS SUBSEQUENTLY ACHIEVED BY ANY PARTICULAR TRADING PROGRAM.

ONE OF THE LIMITATIONS OF HYPOTHETICAL PERFORMANCE RESULTS IS THAT THEY ARE GENERALLY PREPARED WITH THE BENEFIT OF HINDSIGHT. IN ADDITION, HYPOTHETICAL TRADING DOES NOT INVOLVE FINANCIAL RISK, AND NO HYPOTHETICAL TRADING RECORD CAN COMPLETELY ACCOUNT FOR THE IMPACT OF FINANCIAL RISK IN ACTUAL TRADING. FOR EXAMPLE, THE ABILITY TO WITHSTAND LOSSES OR TO ADHERE TO A PARTICULAR TRADING PROGRAM IN SPITE OF TRADING LOSSES ARE MATERIAL POINTS WHICH CAN ALSO ADVERSELY AFFECT ACTUAL TRADING RESULTS. THERE ARE NUMEROUS OTHER FACTORS RELATED TO THE MARKETS IN GENERAL OR TO THE IMPLEMENTATION OF ANY SPECIFIC TRADING PROGRAM WHICH CANNOT BE FULLY ACCOUNTED FOR IN THE PREPARATION OF HYPOTHETICAL PERFORMANCE RESULTS AND ALL OF WHICH CAN ADVERSELY AFFECT ACTUAL TRADING RESULTS

Table of Contents

This book is dedicated to the memory of

My Dad AL who taught me along with

Life's lessons

The importance of investing

And to all my children

May the next generation of investors

Please step up to the plate!

Preface

Congratulations! You have finally decided to get serious about your financial future and are looking for serious results. The *'Shoestring Millionaire' Trading Strategies* are a great first step. *'Shoestring Millionaire'* will give you the tools you need to help you achieve the results you have been looking for. Welcome aboard! I along with my coauthor Chuck Hughes have a lot to share with you! I'm looking forward to sharing easy to learn and even easier to implement investing strategies. These simple strategies will turn even a neophyte investor into a seasoned pro in no time. Chuck will be sharing his own personal tips and strategies that will help all levels of investors reach their goals. He also has a tremendous talent and success in helping the more seasoned investor reach their full potential. I'm very excited about the combination our two knowledge bases and our five simple to learn, simple to implement investing strategies. Together our goal is to give you the best investing strategies available today! So, as my teenagers tell me, "Let's get it started!"

I am a firm believer that everyone regardless of age or level of investment experience should diversify their assets between real estate, stocks and fixed income investments. The table below compares the long-term return performance for Treasury Bills, Treasury Bonds, home prices, and common stocks. The compounded growth of $1,000 invested in each asset class over the past 65 years is depicted below.

Growth of $1,000 Investment Over Last 65 Years

Asset Class	Growth of $1,000	Annual Return	Real Return
Inflation		**4.1%**	
Treasury Bills	**$14,640**	**4.2%**	**0.1%**
Treasury Notes	**$33,520**	**5.6%**	**1.5%**
Home Prices	**$57,485**	**6.4%**	**2.3%**
Common Stocks	**$1,261,758**	**11.6%**	**7.5%**

Type of Asset Class:
Treasury Bills: 30-Day Maturity
Treasury Notes: 5-Year Maturity
Home Prices: Home Price Appreciation (national average)*
Common Stocks: S&P 500 Stock Index

* Data Source: US Census Bureau and National Association of Realtors

> ***"How many millionaires do you know who have become wealthy by investing in savings accounts? I rest my case."***
>
> **Robert G. Allen**

Yet this is how the majority of Americans invest. Unfortunately, this is not the road to carefree retirement or financial freedom. With low interest rates, wealth attainment through this venue is virtually impossible. True, your money is safe. It is as safe as a ship in the harbor but at the same time the ship and your money are going nowhere.

I like most had the miss or maybe fortune of not being born a Rockefeller, DuPont, or Mellon. I was not born with and raised with the knowledge and pressures of how to manage money. What money my family did have was easily managed in the family savings account. I worked hard, but it just wasn't enough. Like most American families we had big expenses, tuition payments, car payments, mortgages and medical expenses. Not to mention a variety of new unforeseen expenditures surrounding 'boomerang' kids and elderly parents. What was left in our 'savings' account was laughable. Retirement was no longer on the horizon. It became a distant and mythical destination. I had to come up with a plan and fast. I put aside a small amount of money that I would start using for investing. I would have liked to start with more but this was all I was willing to risk. I was beginning the journey of my lifetime and I was starting it all on a 'shoestring'.

Hard work and learning have given way to great investing success for me. Through the years I have accumulated a set of tools that have given me the power and confidence to invest with superior results. Like me an investor can start with a small amount of money and learn strategies that will help their money grow into his or her dreams.

Why You Should Invest in Stocks

The S&P 500 Index has long been recognized as the true 'benchmark' to track the performance of the U.S. stock market. The long-term compounded annual return for the S&P 500 Index over the past sixty five years has been 11.6%. This 11.6% annual return far exceeds the 6.4% average home price appreciation over the same period. Over the long-term, residential real estate provided a 'real' annual return of about 2.3% after accounting for inflation which averaged 4.1% over the past sixty five years. Stocks on the other hand provided a 'real' annual return of 7.5% which was three times greater than the real return for real estate. The previous table clearly demonstrates that stocks are the real performance winner when compared to other asset classes and provide the only substantial real return after accounting for inflation.

I consider stock investing different than investing in gold, real estate or collectibles etc. A company that produces earnings and is able to retain those earnings increases the net worth or equity of the company. This increase in net worth creates economic value for stock holders.

As the net worth of the company grows, the company can increase production or services or in the case of a bank the bank can increase its loans. This increase in production or services can in turn create more income for the company. I consider investing in a company that is growing its net worth as a real investment. This is different than buying real estate or gold or antiques with the hope that someone will pay you more than what you paid for it. This is price speculation.

If Most of Your Assets Are Invested In Real Estate or Fixed Income Consider Diversifying into Stocks

While home ownership has provided an excellent return over the long term, I still think that it is prudent for all investors to diversify their assets between real estate, stocks and fixed income investments. If most or all of your assets are invested in real estate consider diversifying into stocks and fixed income investments. I personally have about one-half of my assets invested in real estate and one-half invested in stocks and dividend paying stocks.

Over the Long-Term Stocks are the Clear Winner

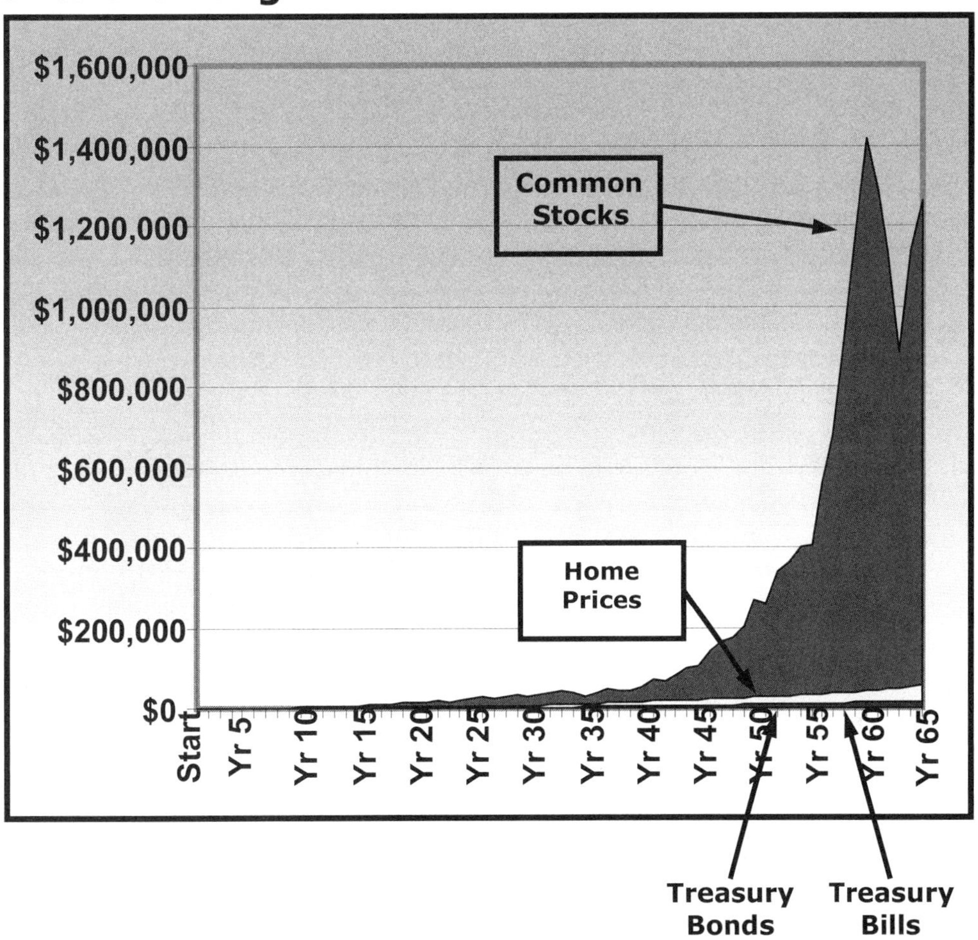

Shoestring Millionaire Performance Results

The goal of this book is to provide you with simple investment strategies that provide superior returns with low risk for that portion of your assets that you dedicate for investment in stocks. The *Shoestring Millionaire Program* consists of a total of five trading strategies with simple rules that in most cases can be implemented in just a few minutes. These strategies are rule based and employ rules that direct you when to enter and exit a trade.

The best quality of these strategies is their simplicity. They can be implemented by the most novice investor as well as the more seasoned investor. The rules highlight when a stock is to be purchased and when it should be sold. All guess work is removed with this rule-based approach. Another plus is that some of the strategies are illustrated with many years of historical performance data. Just like most things in life, history does tend to repeat itself in the financial arena.

Invest with Confidence

You may wonder about the significance of the historical performance data presented in this book for the various strategies and how this historical data is relevant to successful investing today. This historical performance data has demonstrated the consistent profitability and low risk nature of the *Shoestring Millionaire Trading Strategies* and this has given me the confidence to invest one half of my net worth in the strategies.

Following the rules for the *Shoestring Millionaire Trading Strategies* has helped me accumulate $1,051,750.14 in trading profits and income over the past twenty four months. Copies of my brokerage statements and tax schedules are included throughout this book and in the Appendix. This trading income far exceeds my publishing income and I am publishing this book with a genuine desire to help others invest wisely. The *Shoestring Millionaire Trading Strategies* has changed my life and provides my family with financial security.

Don't Get Your Financial Advice from the TV

I'm sure you have all seen market analysts on TV touting their latest stock market prediction or have read books or articles on stock investing. With rare exception, these market analysts don't actually invest in their own recommendations. There is never any accounting or actual track record for all of these predictions because none actually exist. These analysts don't feel the pain when their recommendation incurs a large loss. And they certainly don't follow up with a confession when their prediction goes bad. Talk is cheap. Don't invest your hard-earned money based on a prediction given by someone who does not invest in their own recommendations. I invest in all of the strategies presented in this book and my documented trading income proves that the strategies really work.

I am always amazed by the statistic that the average American spends more time shopping for a car than he or she does planning their financial future. *Shoestring Millionaire Trading* will provide you with an opportunity to take control of your financial future and achieve your financial goals.

My great-great grandfather Lawrence journeyed across the United States as a '49er in hopes of finding his fortune in the California gold rush. Investing is a journey. There are still fortunes to be discovered. Your fortune is out there just waiting to be uncovered. Unlike my ancestors there is no need for perilous travel. You can start your journey right now in the comfort of your own home.

> ***"Success in business (investing) requires training and discipline and hard work. But if you're not frightened by these things, the opportunities are just as great today as they ever were."***
>
> **David Rockefeller**

Let my many years of investment experience guide you and provide the needed training. If you provide the hard work, together we can achieve financial success. I hope you join me on this exciting journey!

All the Best,

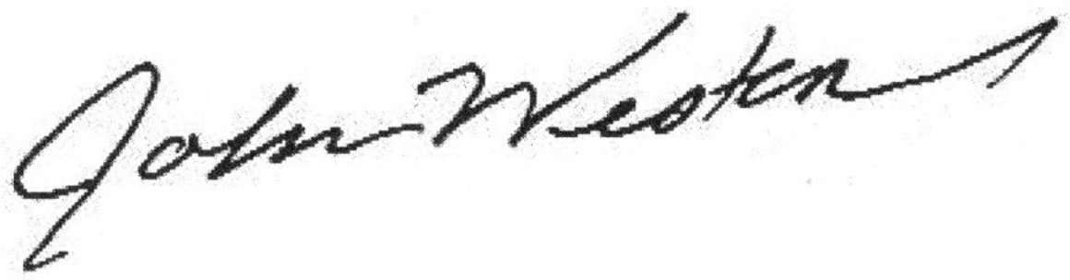

John Weston

Chapter 1

Five Immutable Trading Rules

Every day the consumer is inundated with information on how to invest their money. We see it on TV, hear it on the radio, read about it newspapers, books and on the internet. Every program appears to have a different spin on how to invest successfully. What is a potential investor to do? While the financial press can provide valuable services, this onslaught of investing advice can confuse and potentially misguide even the most experienced investors. Buy, sell or hold? On any given day three different analysts can give you three different opinions on a stock. How does a potential investor process this sometimes conflicting information and implement an investing program that will meet his or her financial goals?

The first premise that investors must understand is that their foundation for a long-term successful investing program should not be based on a methodology that tries to predict the future. No one can consistently predict the future. My experience has taught me to rely on a systematic approach to investing based on historical percentages and probability. The most effective investing approach is to follow a strategy with clear rules that tell you when to 'buy' and when to 'sell'. Such a strategy does not rely on guesswork and emotions.

Get Evenitis

Emotional decision making has caused many investors to make mistakes and is the main obstacle to investors achieving consistent returns on their investments. A good example of these types of mistakes would be the 'loss aversion' tendency of investors to hold on to losing investments instead of cutting losses short. Human nature instinctively finds the concept of loss, no matter how small, very difficult. This tendency causes investors to maintain their losing positions hoping and wishing that somehow the investment will 'turn around' and they can recover their loss and break even. Utilizing a rule based strategy with clearly defined buy and sell rules can help you avoid this common mistake.

> ***"When I have to depend upon hope in a trade I get out of it."***
>
> **Jesse Livermore**

'Could Have', 'Should Have', 'Would Have'

I noticed over the years that investors that rely on guesswork, good stories or predictions to make investing decisions often use the terms 'could have', 'should have' and 'would have'. For example, "I had huge profits on my tech stocks. If I had only sold them before the big collapse I ***'could have'*** made a fortune and retired and led the easy life". Or "My broker talked me into buying XYZ Biotech because it had a promising new drug that would dramatically increase the company profits and provide windfall profits to the lucky investors who owned XYZ Biotech stock. I ***'should have'*** doubled my money but instead I took a large loss when the promising new drug developed by XYZ failed to get FDA approval due to previously unknown side effects".

> ***"In the business world, the rearview mirror is always clearer than the front windshield"***
>
> **Warren Buffett**

Instead of relying on stories or predictions, I would rather invest using a rule based strategy like *Shoestring Millionaire Strategy # 1* that has historically produced a 3,411% percent return over a twenty-four year period enabling you to double your initial investment every year on average. Strategy # 1 has simple buy and sell rules that direct you when to buy a stock and more importantly when to sell. The strategy does not have to rely on 'guessing' future price movement.

Rule # 1 - Rely on a Rule Based Trading Strategy

Emotions tend to control our decision making and can be counterproductive to financial success. Fear and greed are two powerful emotions that can leave an investor feeling powerless. The *Shoestring Millionaire Trading Strategies* can provide investors the essential discipline necessary to overcome the emotional obstacles of fear and greed which prevent investors from making sound decisions.

Rule based strategies remove the reliance of making investing decisions based on guesswork or trying to predict the future. Investors instead make buy and sell decisions determined by strategy rules. Knowing 'when to sell' is one of the more difficult investing decisions and can prevent investors from realizing consistent investment returns if they sell too early because of fear or sell too late because of greed. A good rule based investing strategy will alleviate the problem of knowing when to sell with rules that include 'sell' instructions with every trade.

> ***"In this age of instant information, investors can experience both fear and greed at the exact same moment"***
>
> **Sam Stovall**

Rule # 2 - 'Keep it Simple'

The Teenager Test

All of the strategies presented in this book have passed the 'teenager test'. I explain the strategy to my teenagers and they must be able to understand the strategy and implement the rules in order for the strategy to be included in the *Shoestring Millionaire Trading Program*. The elements of a good trading strategy would include:

1. It is rule based giving the trader no choices or decisions to make
2. The strategy rules tells you when to buy and when to sell
3. Easy to understand
4. Has a long history of profitability in both bull and bear markets
5. Must be low risk

Rule # 3 - Limit Your Losses

In my trading experience, one of the most important trading principles is to limit your losses and let your profits run. A large loss can devastate your financial health and it may take years for you to recover from a large loss. For example, if your portfolio suffered a 50% loss during the last bear market (which was very possible considering the NASDAQ 100 Index lost more than 50% of its value) it would take a subsequent gain of 100% in your portfolio just to break even!

Let's assume you had a $10,000 portfolio that incurred a 50% loss which resulted in the value of your portfolio declining to $5,000. You would then have to achieve a 100% return on your $5,000 portfolio in order break even with the value returning to $10,000. The long term average annual return for the broadly based S&P 500 Index is 11.6%. At that annual return rate it would take 5½ years to recover from a 50% loss.

Rule # 4 - Hold on to Your Winners

Letting your winners run is another important principle for successful portfolio management. Most investors want to do just the opposite and take a quick 10 or 15% profit as soon as they can. It is human nature for people to gain great satisfaction when they win, no matter how great or small that win may be. One only needs to watch parents at youth sports games to verify this theory. Investors will sell early to feel the euphoria associated with winning even when the market conditions are favorable and will allow them to reap greater profits later on.

Most novice investors tend to invest with a limited upside and unlimited downside. They will sell a stock when they have a small profit but continue to hold losing stocks. Eventually they wind up with a portfolio of losers. When you establish a portfolio there is no way to predict which holdings are going to produce big profits over time. Typically, if you own a diversified portfolio of let's say 10 stocks usually there are one or two of the ten stocks that produce a big profit that accounts for most of the gain for the entire portfolio. It's the big winners that Peter Lynch calls "Four Baggers" (stocks that quadruple in value) not the small winners that produce profitable portfolios. You can't tell in advance which of the ten stocks might produce a large profit. So you want to trade with a strategy that continues to hold on to the profitable stocks and sell the losing positions when the strategy rules issue a sell signal.

Rule # 5 - You Must Have a Plan for Down Markets

Most investors do well during a bull market as a 'rising tide lifts all boats'. But most investors are not emotionally prepared for bear markets. Bear markets can be devastating and it may take many years for investors to recover their losses experienced during a bear market. During the 2002 bear market the NASDAQ Index lost 76% of its value. After a 76% loss if this index were to appreciate 12% a year thereafter it would take more than 12 years for the price of the index to return to its starting value. During bear markets many stocks can lose more than 50% of their value. This type of loss is hard for most investors to handle emotionally.

The *Shoestring Millionaire Trading Strategies* are designed to work in any type of market and were profitable during the last two severe bear markets. The *Shoestring Millionaire Strategies* are rule based and can help investors maintain an investing discipline that is necessary to profit during down markets.

Chapter 2

'The Most Powerful Force in Investing'

To the average investor the stock market can seem complicated and confusing. Stocks can go up or down for no apparent reason. Intel reports great earnings but the stock plummets. The price of oil drops and the inflation report is tame but the major stock market indexes dive. Pfizer reports terrible earnings but the stock rallies. The Friday Employment Report is dismal but the Dow Jones Industrial Average soars. When it comes right down to it, the reason *why* stock prices are going up or down seems to be anybody's guess. You might as well try to read tea leaves.

This may sound like 'financial heresy' but ***I really don't care why stock prices move up or down***. Highly paid analysts would have us believe that a company's fundamentals drive stock prices. Yet how many times have you seen the stock of companies with good fundamentals crash while those with terrible fundamentals soar? But none of that matters for one simple reason . . . because at the end of the day, if there are more shares being bought than sold then the price of the stock will go up. And if there are more shares being sold than bought, then the price of the stock will go down. It's just that simple. Everything else is just noise.

To make real money in the market you don't need to know why a stock price rises or falls, you just need to know in advance which way it's most likely to go. If you can quantitatively measure the buying and selling pressure of a stock then you will know in advance whether the price is likely to rally or decline.

Successful trading can be reduced to two simple rules:

1) **Buy investments if the buying pressure exceeds the selling pressure**
2) **Sell investments if the selling pressure exceeds the buying pressure**

The best way to measure buying and selling pressure is to track the price trend of the daily closing price of a stock. If the daily closing price of a stock is increasing then the buying pressure is exceeding selling pressure and the stock should be bought. If the daily closing price of a stock is decreasing then the selling pressure is exceeding buying pressure and the stock should be sold.

One of the most important rules I learned as a novice investor was that you want to purchase a stock only if the buying pressure exceeds selling pressure as indicated by the closing price of the stock trending up.

Trying to profit by investing in a stock with a closing price that is trending down is very difficult as it requires that you correctly predict when the price of the stock will 'bottom out'. This is often referred to as 'trying to catch falling daggers'. Buying a stock because it is cheap and then trying to predict when a stock's price will bottom out can be nearly impossible to forecast correctly on a regular basis. This 'crystal ball' type of approach can leave the investor in a vulnerable position. A safer approach would be to wait until a stock's closing price is in an up trend before investing. Patience will often pay off handsomely if the investor is able to embrace this virtue. A stock's closing price movement reflects all of the known information about a company so let the price movement of the stock tell you when you should invest.

> ***"He who lives by the crystal ball soon learns to eat ground glass"***
>
> **Edgar R Fiedler**

There are hundreds indicators available that help you pick stocks. The more complex an indicator is, the more difficult it is to use and the higher the probability that an error will occur. 'Keep it simple' is my motto. I try to instill this into my life as often as possible. I also try to translate this philosophy into my investing. You can look at formulas that are complicated enough to put a man on the moon or you can keep it simple and look at trend lines that track the closing price of a stock. Trend lines work and are easily understood. That is why I prefer to use them.

> ***"Life is really simple, but men insist on making it complicated"***
>
> **Confucius**

The goal of the *Trend Line Indicator* is to determine whether a stock's closing price is in an up trend or down trend. This has to be established before you invest in a stock. Investing with the trend is a basic principal that is required for successful investing.

Rely on the Trend Instead of Predictions

The best time to invest in a stock is when its upward closing price trend has already been established. Unfortunately, the novice investor tends to purchase 'cheap' stocks that are in a closing price down trend hoping to pick the bottom of the price movement. Stocks that are in a downward closing price trend should be sold. A wise investor will look at the closing price trend for assistance as the closing price trend will reveal in advance which way the stock price is most likely to move. Closing price trends are not predictions. Buying a stock with a closing price down trend is asking the investor to be a forecaster. The studies presented in this Chapter demonstrate that closing price trends tend to continue in the same direction and can continue on longer than one may initially expect.

Measuring Buying & Selling Pressure

Sample 80 Day Trend Line for Reynolds American

The chart below is a one-year daily closing price chart for Reynolds American (RAI) common stock. The horizontal axis at the bottom of the chart references the time period covered by the chart. The vertical axis on the right side of the chart represents the price of RAI stock and in this example ranges from 37.5 to 65. The vertical bars represent the daily trading price range for RAI. To calculate the 80-Day closing price trend line, you would add up the closing prices of RAI for the last 80 days and divide by 80. This average closing price would then be plotted each day on the price chart. Each day you would recalculate the 80-Day closing price average and plot the price again for each day. Eventually you will have a line that represents the 80-Day closing price trend line. The 80-Day closing price trend line for RAI is displayed in the chart below. Of course today you can easily and quickly obtain closing price trend line charts from numerous websites. The 80-Day closing price average for RAI is currently 60.44 which is circled on the far right side of the price chart (Chart courtesy of stockcharts.com.).

Determining a Trend

One of the easiest ways to determine whether a closing price trend is up or down would be to plot a 'fast' trend line and a 'slow' trend line and monitor the crossing of these two trend lines. For example, an up trend would occur if the 40-Day closing price trend line (fast) crossed above the 80-Day closing price trend line (slow). A closing price down trend would occur if the 40-Day trend line (fast) crossed below the 80-Day trend line (slow).

Trend Line Changes

Refer to the Pfizer (PFE) daily price graph below which depicts a 40-Day (fast) closing price trend line and an 80-Day (slow) closing price trend line. The trend lines indicate that PFE stock entered a closing price 'down' trend in May as the 40-Day trend line crosses below the 80-Day trend line at around the 23.50 price level. Selling pressure was exceeding buying pressure. If you owned PFE stock you would want to sell your shares as the closing price trend is 'down' and at this point you don't know how long the price decline will last. The closing price trend reverses to an 'up' trend in August at the 25.75 price level. PFE remains in a closing price 'up' trend as the 40-Day trend line remains above the 80-Day trend line indicating that buying pressure continues to exceed selling pressure. Monitoring the 40-Day and 80-Day trend lines is an easy and effective way to determine the current trend of buying pressure versus selling pressure. Chart courtesy of stockcharts.com.

Constructing a 'Weighted' Trend Line Strategy

'Weighted' trend lines are similar to equally weighted trend lines just discussed except that when you calculate a 'weighted' trend line, more weight is given to the price movement of the more recent days. A rule-based trend line strategy could be constructed by buying a stock when its 40-Day Weighted Trend Line (WTL) crosses above the 80-Day WTL (indicating more buying pressure) and selling a stock when its 40-Day WTL crosses below the 80-Day WTL (more selling pressure). My historical research over a twenty-five year period reveals that 'Weighted' trend line strategies on average produce about 50% more profit and have a higher percentage of winning trades compared to equally weighted trend line strategies which tend to generate more frequent 'false' trend changes. I therefore recommend using weighted trend lines over equally weighted trend lines when determining the closing price trend.

Downloading a 'Weighted' Trend Line Chart

Weighted Trend Line (WTL) Charts can easily be downloaded from a number of financial websites such as Yahoo Finance, BigCharts.com and StockCharts.com. Theses websites automatically calculate weighted trend lines and can display a daily price chart with the 40 and 80-Day Weighted Trend Lines. I recommend that you monitor the 40 and 80-Day WTL for any stocks you own regardless of which investment strategy you use to purchase stocks. If you own a stock and a 'safety switch' sell signal occurs with the 40-Day WTL crossing below the 80-Day WTL then consider selling that stock. Listed below are instructions for obtaining price charts with 40 and 80-Day Weighted Trend Lines from www.stockcharts.com.

Steps for Plotting Weighted Trend Lines for American Eagle from Stock Charts.Com

1. When you log on to the home page of the stockcharts.com website there is a window that allows you to type in a stock symbol. In this example I typed in 'AEOS' the stock symbol for American Eagle and clicked 'GO'. An American Eagle chart then appears.
2. Below the chart display there are several options that allow you to modify the chart (see example on following page).
3. For 'Periods' select daily. For 'Style' select OHLC. Select 'OFF' for Volume which is not needed.
4. For 'Duration' select 1 Year or 2 Year. Usually the 1 Year or 2 Year selection is a sufficient time span to include the latest 40/80-Day trend line cross over
5. For 'Price Overlays' select Exp Mov. Avg 40 on the first line which will produce the 40-Day Weighted Trend Line and on the second line select Exp Mov. Avg 80 which will produce the 80-Day Trend Weighted Line
6. For 'Indicator' Windows select None as they are not needed
7. Select 'Update Chart' and a chart similar to the AEOS chart on the following page will appear
8. You can then change the symbol and select 'Update Chart' and a new Weighted Trend Line chart will be created.
9. Bookmark this web page and the chart settings will be saved for future analysis

Stock Charts.Com Chart Service

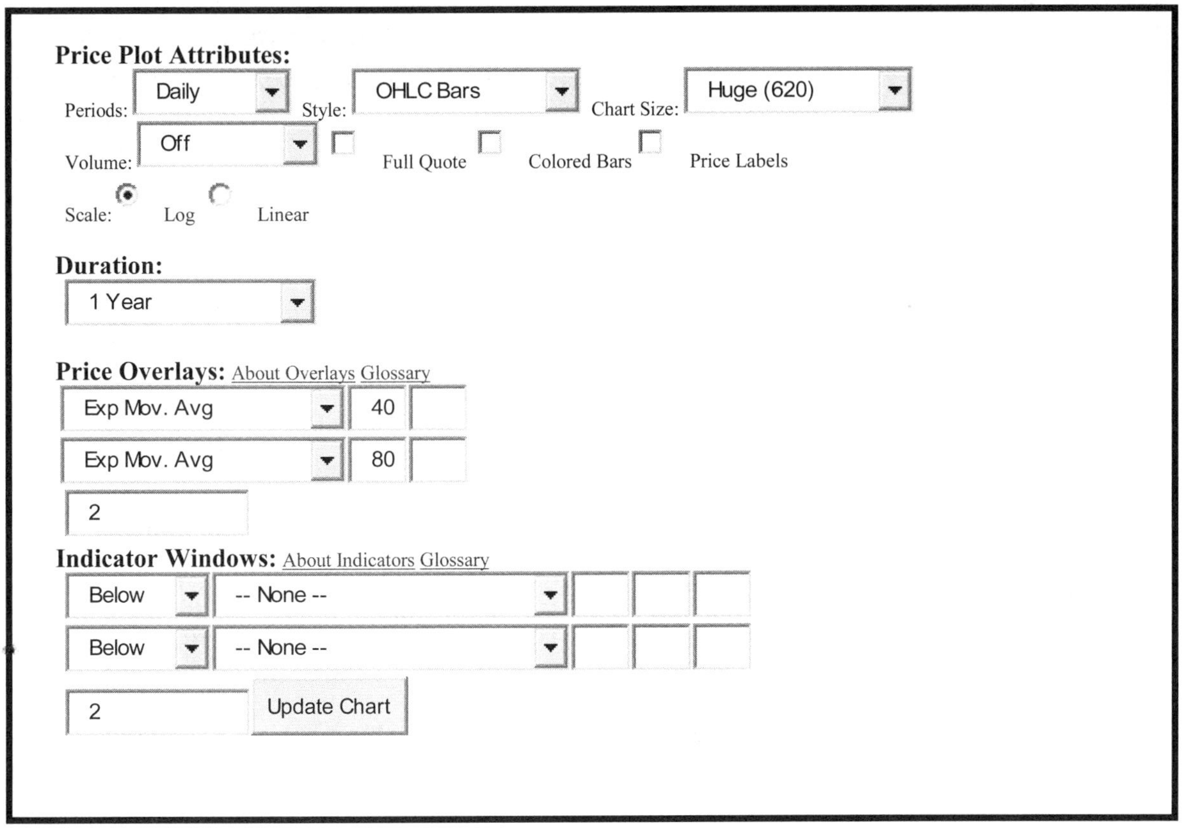

American Eagle 1-Year Weighted Trend Line Chart

The 1-Year chart that follows displays the American Eagle (AEOS) daily price and the 40 and 80-Day Weighted Trend Lines obtained from stockcharts.com following the steps listed on the previous page. The 40-Day Weighted Trend Line crossed above the 80-Day WTL in January (buying pressure exceeded selling pressure) at the 26.00 price level signaling a 'buy' for AEOS stock. On the day this chart was created the 40-Day WTL remained above the 80-Day WTL and AEOS continues in a closing price uptrend. Sell AEOS stock if the 40-Day WTL crosses below the 80-Day WTL.

If you want to look at another stock chart then simply change the symbol and click 'Update Chart' and a new chart will be created. Don't forget to bookmark this page on your web browser so that the settings are saved for future use. This is a quick and easy way to obtain a Weighted Trend Line chart that gives us an instant 'picture' of the trend for the stock selected. Chart courtesy of stockcharts.com.

American Eagle 1-Year Weighted Trend Line Chart

Measuring Closing Price Movement Is the 'Key' to Developing a Profitable Strategy

The stock market is in a constant state of flux. The constant up and down price movement of a stock makes it difficult at times to see the real price trend of an individual stock. That is why it is important for the potential investor to become comfortable with trend lines. The cross over of the 40 and 80-Day trend lines can give us a quick and accurate overview of an individual stock's current closing price trend. It can tell us if the stock is in a healthy up trend or in a less desirable down trend. Sometimes a stock's price movement is 'flat lined' and there is no clear trend. In order to be a successful investor we do not have to know what an analyst's rating is for a stock or if there is 'insider' buying. All of that information is reflected in a stock's closing price movement which can be quantitatively measured by a trend line.

Trading with the Closing Price Trend

How many times have you been tempted to buy a stock based on a news clip, or a story you heard at a party of Joe 'hitting it big'? I've learned over the years that most of these are just that, stories. A lot of times these stories are based on mythical earnings, legend, 'insider information' and perhaps one too many cocktails. Learn patience. If you learn no other skill in investing learn this one. Patience will keep you from the temptation of buying a stock in a price down trend. It will keep you from purchasing the 'sure thing' stock that continues to spiral down in price.

Please take this advice. I know, as my kids say "been there, done that". I've been there. I've purchased stocks in a down trend and have lived to regret it. Buy when buying pressure exceeds selling pressure, and sell when selling pressure exceeds buying pressure. That is profitable investing in its simplest form.

'Safety Switch'

Investors who use trend lines as a guideline to enter and exit trades can often save themselves from large losses by selling a stock when its 40-Day trend line crosses below its 80-Day trend line. This trend line cross over to the downside acts as a 'safety switch' that warns investors that for whatever reason a stock has just entered a closing price down trend and should be sold.

Following a discipline of selling stocks when a 'safety switch' sell signal occurs enables investors to 'lock in' profits and practice prudent money management which reduces the overall risk of your financial investment program. Once a 'safety switch' sell signal occurs it is difficult to predict how long the down trend in a stock will persist and how severe the price decline in a stock will be. The best policy is to sell the stock in case the stock experiences a severe price decline which can endanger your financial health. And wait until the subsequent price movement tells you the stock has returned to an up trend before you invest in the stock again.

The charts that follow contain two examples of 'safety switch' sell signals for Nortel Networks and Sun Microsystems. These are good examples of how the 'safety switch' can prevent devastating losses that could require years of additional investing just to recover your initial investment and break even.

Nortel Networks

Created with SuperCharts by Omega Research © 1997

Sun Microsystems

There Are Always Stocks in Up Trends Even During a Bear Market

Many investors suffered painful losses during the last two severe bear markets as they were fully invested in stocks at the peak. At the beginning of down turns very few investors can imagine the extent of the losses that occur by the end of the bear market. There is never a good time to take a loss but a loss later on in life can be quite devastating and lead to uncertainty about the future. This Chapter is dedicated to helping investors avoid any potential large losses in the future by using the trend line exit rule presented here. I want us all to learn the *Trend Line* philosophy for wise investing and avoid the mistakes of the past. If you learn nothing else from this book at least learn to cut your losses before they grow too large.

> ***"Mistakes are the usual bridge between inexperience and wisdom"***
>
> **Phyllis Therous**

Since the *Shoestring Millionaire Trading Strategies* are rule based they help to eliminate investing decisions based on predictions, trying to guess future price movement and 'tips'. The focus of a rule based strategy is to help decrease risk and stress.

Remember from Chapter 1 that it takes a 100% gain just to 'break even' from a 50% loss. We also learned that one of the cardinal rules of profitable investing is to cut losses short and let your profits run. The *Shoestring Millionaire Trend Line Strategy* is designed to do just that. With the *Trend Line Strategy* you will be able to tell immediately whether a stock should be purchased or sold. I am not saying there will never be losses. There is always risk in any investment. The investor understands and takes on that burden in hopes of receiving a higher return. That is why it is just as important to learn how and when to cut losses short as it is to learn when to let your profits roll on. The *Trend Line Strategy* gives you clear and concise buy and sell signals and informs you in advance the most likely direction of future price movement.

> ***"Whales only get harpooned when they come to the surface and turtles can only move forward when they stick their neck out but investors face risk no matter what they do"***
>
> **Charles A Jaffe**

Most investors cringe at the thought of a bear market. The *Shoestring Millionaire Trend Line Strategy* historical profit results presented in following Chapters will demonstrate that during the last three bear markets, the *Trend Line Strategy* was able to prevent an 'Investing Tsunami'. Not only was financial peril avoided, but the *Trend Line Strategy* was able to ride the wave to profits. Can we change the direction of the market? No, but we can change our course and find stocks that may have been overlooked and neglected in the past but are currently in a trend line bull mode.

The stock graphs that follow are just a few of the hundreds of examples of stocks that were in a *Trend Line Strategy* 'buy mode' during a bear market. These stocks produced substantial profits during periods of excessive stock declines. At any given time somewhere there is a bull market out there . . . . Let the *Trend Line Strategy* help you find it!

Once you learn to interpret trend lines you can use this knowledge to trade a wide variety of investment strategies, many of which we will review in the following Chapters.

Anheuser Busch

Hudson City Bancorp

Unitedhealth Group

Created with SuperCharts by Omega Research © 1997

Chapter 3

'The Best Profit Opportunity of Our Lifetime'

My extensive research of market historical data over the years has led to the discovery of the vast profit opportunity available from investing in small cap stocks. This discovery reveals that small cap stocks provide the best investment returns compared to all other types of investments. Market value or capitalization (cap) is calculated by multiplying the price of the stock by the number of shares outstanding. The table below compares the growth of a $10,000 investment for various investments over the past 65 years. This table dramatically reveals that micro and small cap stocks out perform all other investments by a wide margin. ***A $10,000 investment in small cap value stocks grew to an incredible 490 million dollars over the past 65 years!***

Over the same period a $10,000 investment in micro cap stocks grew to more than 100 million dollars demonstrating that micro and small cap stocks provide the best profit opportunities available today. By comparison, a $10,000 investment in large cap stocks grew to $12,617,580, single family homes $574,850, government bonds $335,200, T-Bills $146,400 and a $10,000 investment in gold grew to $132,850.

Growth of $10,000 Investment

Small Cap Value Stocks	**$490,123,460**
Micro Cap Stocks	**$102,909,840**
Large Cap Stocks	**$12,617,580**
Home Prices	**$574,850**
Government Bonds	**$335,200**
T-Bills	**$146,400**
Gold	**$132,850**

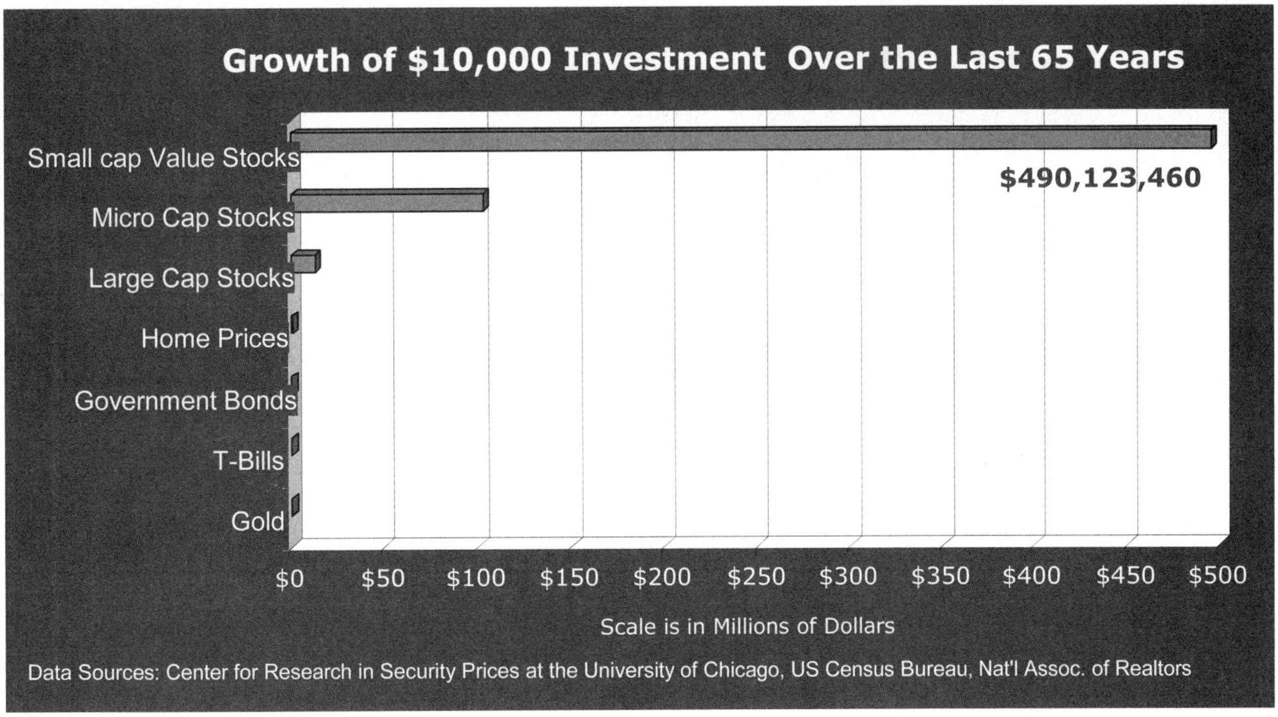

Out Performance of Small Cap Value Stocks *

Profit Comparisons of $10,000 Investment	
Small Cap Value vs Large Cap	39 to 1
Small Cap Value vs Home Prices	861 to 1
Small Cap Value vs Gov't Bonds	1,477 to 1
Small Cap Value vs T-Bills	3,382 to 1
Small Cap Value vs Gold	3,727 to 1

An investment in small cap value stocks outperformed single family home prices by an 861 to 1 margin. These results clearly demonstrate that small and micro-cap stocks are unquestionably the best profit opportunity of our lifetime!

* Small cap stocks are defined as the smallest 30% of market capitalization stocks traded on the NYSE, AMEX and NASDAQ exchanges. Value stocks are defined as the top 30% of stocks with the highest book to price ratios (within the small cap grouping) traded on the NYSE, AMEX and NASDAQ exchanges.

Why Stocks Are the Best Investment

We can see from the previous investment comparison table that stocks provide the best returns when compared to all other types of investments. A $10,000 investment in small cap value stocks provided 1,477 times more profit than US Government Bonds, 3,382 times more profit than T-Bills and 3,727 times more profit than gold.

Companies that produce and retain earnings enable stocks to provide the best returns compared to all other types of investments. Retained earnings increase stock holder's equity also called net worth and makes a company's stock more valuable. This increase in net worth creates economic value for stock holders. As the net worth of a company grows, the company can increase production or services or in the case of a bank can increase loans. This increase in production or services can in turn create more income for the company. A company that is growing its net worth is creating real wealth. Owning equity or stock in such a company is considered a 'real' investment. This is different than buying real estate or precious metals or collectibles with the hope that someone will pay you more than what you paid for it. This is price speculation as there is no growth of net worth or equity in these types of investments.

The increase in stock holder's equity or net worth of a company has always allowed stock investors to enjoy the highest investment returns. As long as companies continue to produce and retain earnings, stock investing will always provide superior returns compared to all other types of investing.

The Small Cap Phenomena

My research of stock performance data also shows that the ***size of a company is the most reliable forecaster of future investment returns***. On average, small companies have higher investment returns than large companies. The relationship between company size and future investment returns covers the entire size spectrum and is not limited to the smallest stocks. Historical return data shows that average investment returns increase as one moves from the largest companies to the smallest. This correlation suggests that past annual returns are of value in predicting future annual returns. Small and micro-cap stocks have continually provided higher investment returns than large cap stocks since 1940 and based on historical correlations should continue to do so in the future.

The table that follows depicts investment returns relative to the size of a company over the past 65 years. This table clearly demonstrates the inverse relationship between the size of a company and investment return with the largest companies producing the lowest returns and the smallest companies producing the highest returns.

> ***"Small opportunities are often the beginning of great enterprises"***
>
> **Demosthenes**

Size Is the Most Reliable Forecaster Of Future Investment Returns

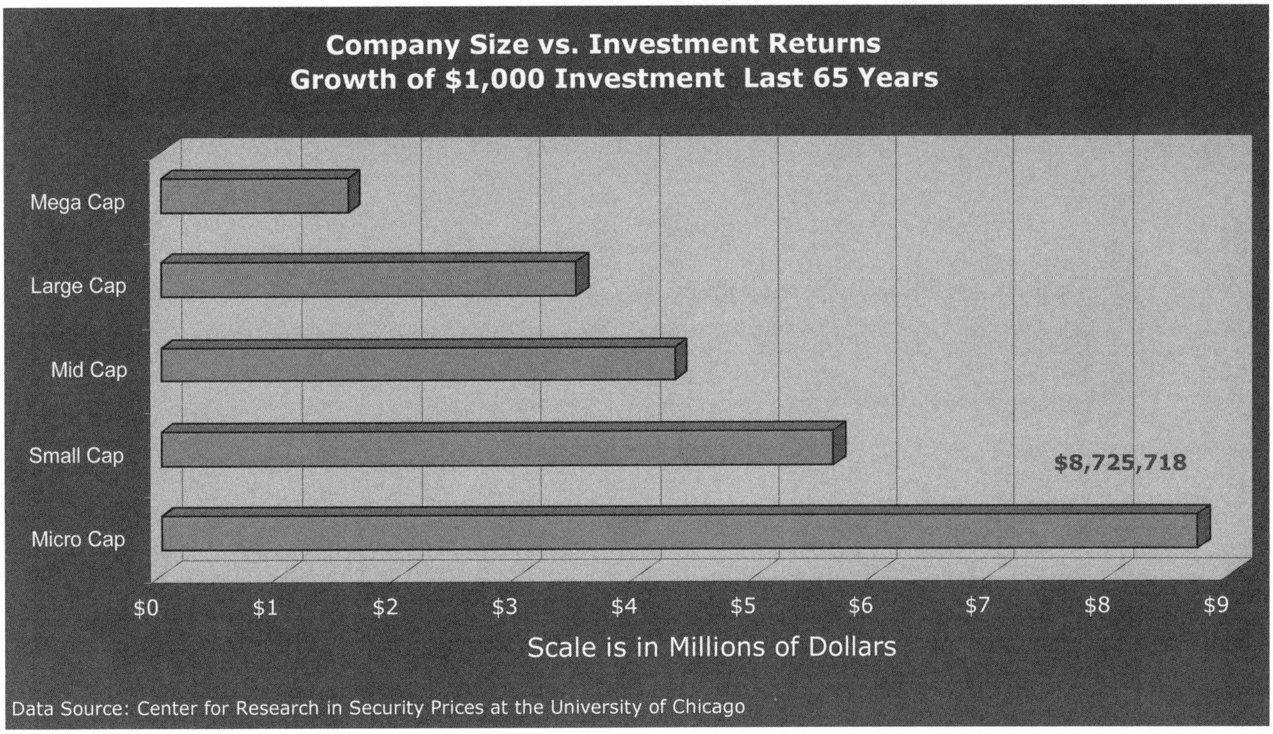

Mega Cap is defined as stocks in the 1st and 2nd Deciles (largest 20%) in terms of market capitalization of stocks traded on NYSE/AMEX/NASDAQ. Large Cap consists of stocks in the 3rd and 4th Deciles, Mid Cap consists of stocks in the 5th and 6th Deciles, Small Cap consists of stocks in the 7th and 8th Deciles and Micro Cap consists of stocks in the 9th and 10th Deciles (smallest 20%) of stocks traded on the NYSE/AMEX/NASDAQ.

'The Law of Large Numbers'

Small companies are able to grow their earnings much faster than large companies and as a result small companies have continually provided better investment returns than large companies over the past 65 years. It is much more difficult for large companies to gain earnings momentum due to the sheer size of their operations. For example, Exxon Mobil (XOM) is a large energy company with a market capitalization of 369 billion dollars (billion with a 'b'). Despite one of the strongest bull markets in history for energy stocks, Exxon was only able to grow its earnings 10% over the past year. Exxon had a net income of 36.6 billion dollars over the past year. 'The Law of Large Numbers' suggests that the size of Exxon Mobil will limit its earnings growth. It would be very difficult for Exxon to achieve 50% annual earnings growth as it would have to increase its net income by 18.3 billion dollars. Many smaller companies, however, can grow their earnings at a 50% or higher annual rate.

> ***"The world is changing very fast. Big will not beat small anymore. It will be the fast beating the slow."***
>
> **Rupert Murdoch**

Investing in small companies that are growing their earnings quickly offers investors a much better opportunity for sizeable investment returns. For example, Omni Energy Services (OMNI) is a small cap energy services company with a market capitalization of 88 million dollars. Omni has an annual earnings growth rate of 650% and as a result has rewarded its shareholders with a 303% stock return over the past year. Exxon Mobil, on the other hand, has only provided its investors with an 8.3% investment return over the same period (including dividends) even though oil prices have nearly doubled over the same period.

Large Versus Small

Company	Market	Earnings	Investment
	Cap	Growth	Return
Exxon Mobil	$369 Billion	10%	8%
Omni Energy	$88 Million	650%	303%

Investing in the major oil companies has produced good returns over the past year but the 'Law of Large Numbers' limits their growth potential. Investing in the small oil and natural gas exploration companies that are growing their earnings quickly offers investors a much better opportunity for sizeable capital gains during this energy bull market. For example, the table below shows that the average return for the sampling of five major oil companies over the past year was 18.2%. This is a decent annual return but the average return over the same period for the sampling of five small cap energy stocks listed below was 1,095%. Small companies that explore and drill for oil and natural gas are able to grow their earnings much faster than large companies and as a result small companies have always provided better investment returns than large companies.

One Year Return

Large Cap	1 Year		Small Cap	1 Year
Energy COs	Return		Energy Companies	Return
Exxon Mobil	8%		Omni Energy	303%
Chevron Texaco	13%		Houston Energy	311%
ConocoPhillips	18%		CANWEST Petroleum	1546%
BP Amoco	20%		Strata Oil & Gas	3167%
Sunoco	33%		National Energy	150%
Average Return	18%		Average Return	1,095%

Next we will examine a strategy for investing in small cap stocks.

Chapter 4

A Powerful Combination

While stock investing provides superior returns compared to all other types of investments, the stock market periodically experiences corrections and bear markets. These corrections and bear markets are unavoidable as there is no way to predict when they will occur and how long they will last. There is a way to profit during both bull and bear markets, however, if we limit our investing to stocks that are in a price 'up trend'. In Chapter 2 we learned that the *Trend Line Indicator (TLI)* measures a stock's closing price movement and determines whether a stock is in a closing price 'up trend' or price 'down trend'. The TLI can be used as a filter by only purchasing stocks that are in a closing price up trend and selling stocks once they enter a closing price down trend. My trading experience confirms that this simple but effective filter not only produces more profits than a 'buy and hold' strategy but it also incurs less risk as stocks in a price 'down trend' are avoided.

Measuring the closing price movement of a stock indicates the current buying and selling pressure occurring in the trading of a stock. This allows us to know in advance the most likely future price direction of a stock. Investing with the closing price trend increases your probability of success and helps avoid large losses by selling stocks when a 'Safety Switch' sell signal occurs. In Chapter 1 we learned that one of the immutable rules of profitable investing is to cut losses short and let your profits run. The *Trend Line Strategy* is designed to do just that. You will be able to tell immediately weather a stock should be bought or sold.

A Powerful Combination

We also learned in Chapter 3 that a company's size is the most reliable forecaster of future investment returns with small cap stocks providing better investment returns than mid and large cap stocks. These small cap returns assume that you use a 'buy and hold' approach to investing during both bull and bear markets. Using the *Trend Line Indicator* to only buy small cap stocks in a closing price 'up trend' can further increase your profits and reduce risk while investing in the asset class with the greatest profit potential. Investing with the trend in the most profitable of all investment classes results in a 'Powerful Combination' that has helped me to produce $1,051,750.14 in actual profits over the past 24 months.

> ***"I am no longer an advocate of elaborate techniques of security analysis in order to find superior value opportunities."***
>
> **Benjamin Graham**

Small Cap Stock Strategy Rules

(Strategy # 1)

Select a small cap stock *
Purchase a small cap stock if its 40-Day Weighted Trend Line (WTL) is above the 80-Day WTL
Sell any stock if the price of the stock declines 15% or more from the entry price or if the 40-Day WTL crosses below the 80-Day WTL whichever occurs first

Small Cap Stock Strategy Example

Actuate Corp (ACTU) is a small cap stock with a market cap of 228 million$. This qualifies ACTU as a small cap stock (see small cap definition below) and satisfies Rule # 1. The ACTU 40-Day Weighted Trend Line (WTL) is currently above its 80-Day WTL which satisfies Rule # 2. ACTU is currently trading at 4.24. If you have $300 to invest then enter an online order or give your broker an order to buy 70 shares of ACTU with a limit order of 4.24 ($300 divided by 4.24 = 70). Enter a 'Good Until Cancelled' (GTC) protective stop order to sell 70 shares of UTX at 3.60 'stop' which is 15% below the 4.24 entry price (4.24 X .85 = 3.60). Enter an online order or give your broker an order to sell 70 shares of ACTU at 3.60 on a stop, 'Good Until Cancelled' (GTC). This order will not be executed unless the price of ACTU stock drops to 3.60.

If the ACTU 40-Day WTL crosses below the 80-Day WTL triggering a 'safety switch' sell signal for ACTU stock, then enter an online order or give your broker an order to sell your 70 shares of ACTU. If this sell signal occurs before ACTU drops to 3.60 then remember to cancel your protective stop order to sell ACTU at 3.60. Wait until the ACTL 40-Day WTL crosses above its 80-Day WTL before considering a new purchase.

* The Russell Investment Group created and maintains the Russell 2000 Index ® which is the most widely used small cap stock benchmark. The table below is an excerpt from the Russell website that lists the market cap data for the Russell 2000 Index ® of small cap stocks. Currently the average market cap for the index is 1.08 billion$ and the largest company has a market cap of 2.375 billion$. Therefore a small cap stock will be defined as a company with less than 2.375 billion$ in market capitalization. The market capitalization of a stock can easily be obtained online from various market data websites such as Bloomberg.com, marketwatch.com and Yahoo Finance.

MONTHLY DATA

Capitalization (in billions)										
Average Market Cap($-WTD)										1.08
Largest Company by Market Cap										2.375
Smallest Company by Market Cap										0.104

Small Cap Stock Strategy Historical Results

There is not much historical data available for many small cap stocks as many small cap stocks started trading recently after their initial public offering. I use the *Omega Super Charts Program* to perform historical return analysis for the *Small Cap Stock Strategy.* The *Super Charts Program* does historical profit calculations using the *Small Cap Stock Strategy* rules of purchasing a small cap stock when its 40-Day Weighted Trend Line (WTL) crosses above the 80-Day WTL and selling a stock when its 40-Day WTL crosses below its 80-Day WTL. Historical testing was limited to small cap stocks that are currently included in the Russell 2000 Index ® of small cap stocks.

Fourteen Years of Historical Results

Listed on the following page are the *Small Cap Stock Strategy* historical profit results for a broad cross section of small cap stocks in virtually every industry sector over a recent fourteen year period. Results are based on initially investing $200 in each stock for the first 'buy' signal and compounding the results thereafter and do not include commissions. This sampling includes both growth and value stocks. You may not recognize many of the names of the small stocks used in this testing but that can be a benefit as investing in small cap stocks will allow you to broaden your investing horizons.

Double Your Initial Investment Every Year

Historical results reveal that the *Small Cap Stock Strategy* produced impressive profits with very low risk. The total initial capital required to invest $200 in each of the fifty stocks tested was $10,000. The total profits realized were $341,149 which translates to a 3,411% return on the initial $10,000 investment. Over the test period this return rate allows you to double your initial investment every year on average if you let your initial investment compound.

The average profit factor over the test period was 18.7 which translates to more than 18 dollars of profit for each 1 dollar of loss. The profit factor is calculated by dividing the total losses by the total profits and is a good measure of risk. A high profit factor indicates that the *Small Cap Stock Strategy* keeps losses to a minimum by exiting losing trades before a big loss occurs and maintaining winning trades as long as the stock remains in a closing price up trend. You may recall from Chapter 1 that one of the basic Rules for profitable investing is to cut losses short and allow your winners to run. The *Small Cap Stock Strategy* almost always exits a trade before a big loss occurs and provides you with the discipline necessary to become a successful investor.

Keep in mind that three bear markets occurred during this period including the worst bear market since 1932 during which the S&P 500 Index and the NASDAQ lost more than 50% of their value. These performance results demonstrate that the *Small Cap Stock Strategy* is a versatile, effective method for profiting in any type of market. The *Small Cap Stock Strategy* can also be used to trade options so in the next Chapter we will examine the 'ins and outs' of put and call options.

Small Cap Stock Strategy Historical Results

Company	Initial Investment	Percent Return	Total Profit	Profit Factor
Badger Meter	$200	1760%	$3,520	3.9
Rackable Systems	$200	155%	$310	56.9
Downey Financial	$200	3848%	$7,696	2.2
Alexanders	$200	2648%	$5,297	5.0
Brocade Communications	$200	587%	$1,174	8.0
CDI Corp	$200	4842%	$9,684	2.0
Ditech	$200	734%	$1,467	7.3
Safety Insurance	$200	213%	$427	74.0
American Science	$200	844%	$1,689	2.3
True Religion Apparel	$200	794%	$1,588	25.9
FTI Consulting	$200	1193%	$2,387	3.2
ATP Oil & Gas	$200	736%	$1,472	9.4
R&G Financial	$200	891%	$1,781	11.7
Amedisys	$200	1053%	$2,107	4.6
Encore Wire	$200	1580%	$3,159	9.5
Aaron Rents	$200	1061%	$2,123	4.0
Technitrol	$200	11865%	$23,731	2.2
Adaptec	$200	3592%	$7,185	7.5
Tower Group	$200	189%	$378	100.0
Amcol Inc	$200	2967%	$5,933	2.3
CMGI Inc	$200	26653%	$53,306	49.1
Andersons Inc	$200	707%	$1,413	20.3
Credit Accept Corp	$200	1037%	$2,074	3.8
Bank Rate Inc	$200	3003%	$6,007	9.8
Bankunited	$200	920%	$1,840	3.8
RLI Corp	$200	3415%	$6,831	2.7
Advent Software	$200	645%	$1,290	4.5
Bally Technologies	$200	3607%	$7,215	5.1
California Coastal	$200	698%	$1,395	100.0
Federal Agriculture Mtg	$200	1991%	$3,983	3.2
AAON Inc	$200	4743%	$9,485	4.9
Daktronics	$200	4806%	$9,611	77.1
Raven Industries	$200	8770%	$17,540	12.9
Americanwest Bancorp	$200	551%	$1,103	12.0
Banta Corp	$200	1641%	$3,282	2.3
Giant Industries	$200	1183%	$2,366	7.0
Safeguard Scientific	$200	13135%	$26,269	5.6
Actuant Corp	$200	3115%	$6,231	2.7
CNS Inc	$200	2282%	$4,564	3.9
Bank Mutual	$200	295%	$590	100.0
Accredited Home Lenders	$200	287%	$575	9.4
Capital Southwest	$200	1797%	$3,593	5.6
Diodes Inc	$200	8611%	$17,222	9.2
Belden Inc	$200	910%	$1,820	2.6
Dynamic Materials	$200	6120%	$12,240	6.6
Comtech Telecom	$200	3858%	$7,716	3.9
Bucyrus Int'l	$200	162%	$323	100.0
Doral Financial	$200	6542%	$13,085	20.9
American Vanguard	$200	14089%	$28,178	2.2
Bel Fuse	$200	3448%	$6,897	2.0
Totals / Averages	**$10,000**	**3411%**	**$341,149**	**18.7**

Examples Of Small Cap Stocks in a Trend Line 'Buy' Signal

(Charts Courtesy of StockCharts.com)

Chapter 5

The Ins and Outs of Puts and Calls

The focus of this Chapter is to teach you the basics of option investing. In my experience, investing in options has been one of the most versatile and rewarding approaches to profitable investing. Option investing enables many different types of investors to achieve their specific investment goals. I have traded many types of option strategies with different investment goals. I favor the four option strategies listed below as I have had good success trading these strategies.

1) Purchase options to realize trading profits
2) Construct an option spread that can profit during an up or down market
3) Sell option premium to produce income
4) An option strategy that protects your stocks from price declines by using dividends to purchase an 'insurance policy' that limits your risk

Important Note: *It is important to note that if you trade the strategies presented in this book, your risk is strictly limited and you can't lose more money than you invest. This is different than trading Forex or futures contracts which can result in a total loss of your account balance and which can force you to receive margin calls that can far exceed the total value of your trading account.*

Learning the mechanics of option investing can be a bit overwhelming particularly if you have never invested in options before. This Chapter is designed as a 'stepping stone' to mastering the option strategies presented in this. As such it can be used as a future reference when learning an option strategy. It is therefore not necessary to memorize all of the material presented in this Chapter.

Let's start with the basics. Options are contracts. The terms of option contracts are standardized and give the buyer the right to buy or sell the underlying stock at a fixed price which is known as the 'strike price'. Option contracts are valid for a specific period of time which ends on option expiration day. All options contracts traded on U.S. Securities Exchanges are issued, guaranteed and cleared by the Options Clearing Corporation (OCC). The OCC is a registered clearing corporation with the Securities and Exchange Commission (SEC) and has received an 'AAA' credit rating from Standard & Poors Corporation for its ability to fulfill its obligations as counter-party for option trades.

There are two types of options; calls and puts. Simply stated a call option is a contract that gives you the right to buy a stock at a specified price which is called the 'strike price' on or before the expiration date of the option. A put option is a contract that gives you the right to sell a stock at a specified price called the 'strike price' on or before the expiration date of the option.

There are two ways to invest in options:

Buying options

Selling short options

Buying Options

The goal of buying an option is to 'Buy Low and Sell High'. Buying a call option is a bullish strategy as the value of a call option will increase as the price of the underlying stock increases. Conversely, if the price of the underlying stock decreases then the value of a call option also decreases.

Buying a put option is a bearish strategy as the value of a put option will increase as the price of the underlying stock decreases. Conversely, if the price of the underlying stock increases then the value of a put option will decrease.

The price you pay for an option is called the premium. When you buy an option, cash is deducted from your brokerage account to pay for the option premium. One option contract normally controls one hundred shares of the underlying stock. Purchasing an option with a 4.00 point premium would result in $400 being deducted from your brokerage account to pay for the premium (4.00 x 100 shares = $400). If you later sold this option for 6.00 points you would realize a $200 profit.

Buy at 4.00 and sell at 6.00 = 2.00 Profit

Conversely, if you later sell this option for 3.00 points you would realize a $100 loss.

Buy at 4.00 and sell at 3.00 = 1.00 Loss

Note: When you buy an option, you can sell the option any time prior to option expiration.

Selling Short Options

The goal of selling short an option is to 'Sell High and Buy Low'. When you sell an option, cash is credited to your brokerage account. For example, if you sell an option for 6.00 points, $600 will be credited to your account ($6.00 x 100 shares = $600). This is just the opposite of purchasing an option. As noted previously, buying an option for 6.00 points would result in $600 being deducted from your account.

Selling a call option is a bearish strategy. An investor who sells a call option is also known as the 'writer'. Selling a call is also known as being 'short' a call. The value of a call option declines as the underlying stock decreases in price. Being 'short' a call option generates profits as the call option decreases in value.

If you sell short a call option and the call option subsequently decreases in price then you can 'buy back' the short call at a lower price which will result in a profit for the call writer (Sell high and buy low). For example, if you sell a call option for 5.00 points and then later buy the call back for 3.00 points you would realize a 2.00 point profit.

Sell call at 5.00 and then buy back at 3.00 = 2.00 profit

This is a similar concept to 'shorting' a stock. If you short a stock that drops in price and then subsequently buy the stock back at a lower price you would realize a profit. For example, if you short Apple stock (AAPL) at 74.25 and subsequently buy the stock back at 70.00 you would realize a 4.25 point profit.

Sell Apple stock at 74.25 and buy back at 70.00 = 4.25 profit

If you sell short a call option for 5.00 points and then later buy the call back at a higher price let's say 7.00 points you would realize a 2.00 point loss.

Sell call at 5.00 and then buy back at 7.00 = 2.00 loss

Selling short a put option is a bullish strategy. An investor who sells short a put option is also known as the 'writer'. Selling short a put is also known as being 'short' a put. The value of a put option declines as the underlying stock increases in price. If you sell a put option and the underlying stock subsequently increases in price then you can 'buy back' the short put at a lower price which will result in a profit for the put writer. For example, if you sell short a put option for 5.00 points and then later buy the put back for 3.00 points you would realize a 2.00 point profit.

Sell put at 5.00 and then buy back at 3.00 = 2.00 profit.

If you sell short a put option for 5.00 points and then later buy the put back at a higher price let's say 7.00 points you would realize a 2.00 point loss.

Sell short put at 5.00 and then buy back at 7.00 = 2.00 loss

Let's review the types of option orders that you would give to your broker (or online) to make sure you understand this important concept.

Order		Result
Buy Call to Open		Establishes Long Call Position
Buy Put to Open		Establishes Long Put Position
Sell Call to Close		Closes Out Long Call Position
Sell Put to Close		Closes Out Long Put Position
Sell Call to Open		Establishes Short Call Position
Sell Put to Open		Establishes Short Put Position
Buy Call to Close		Closes Out Short Call Position
Buy Put to Close		Closes Out Short Put Position

Examples of Online Option Orders

Examples of online brokerage account option orders follow. The first example is a 'buy to open' order to purchase the Microsoft Mar 38-strike call option at the market. This would result in buying the call option.

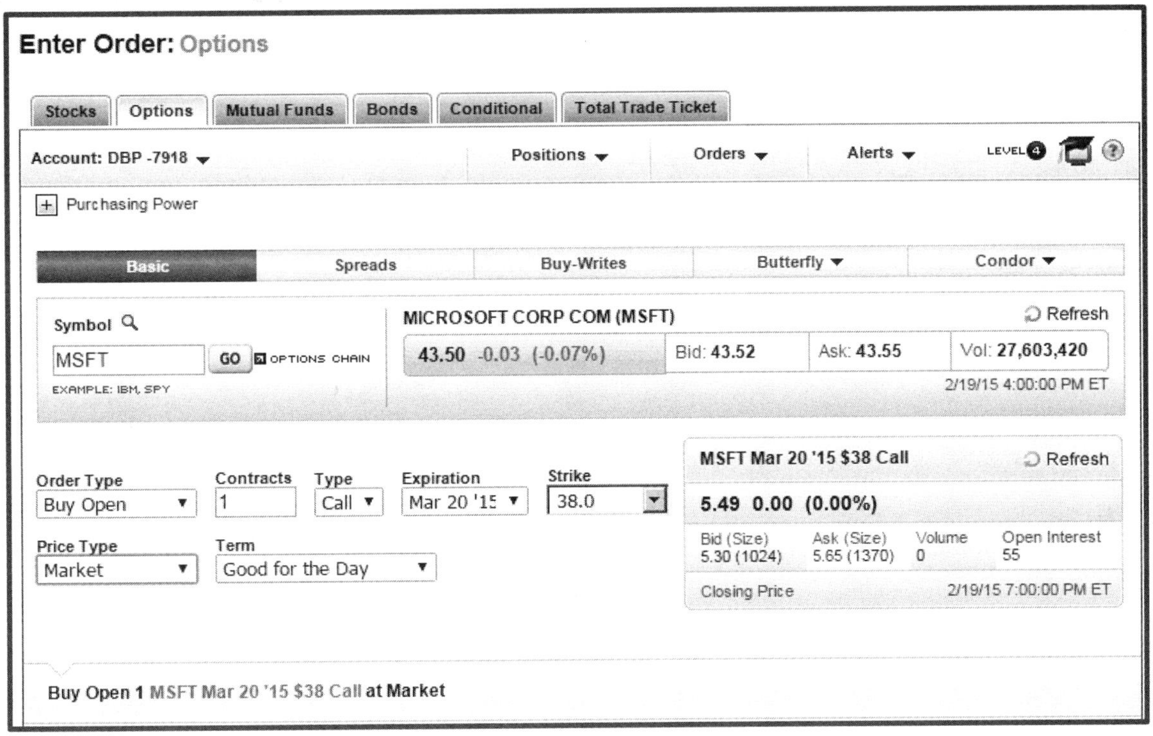

The order below is a 'sell to close' order to close out the Microsoft Mar 38-strike call option at the market. This would result in closing out the call option.

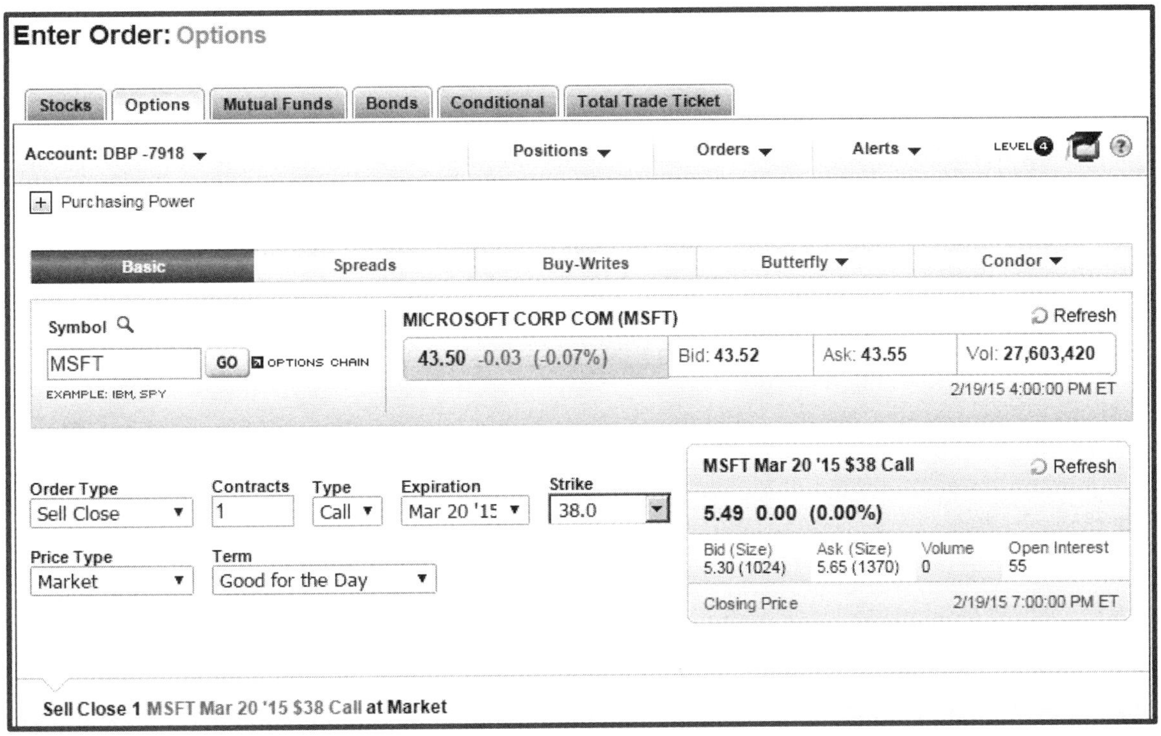

We sell short or sell to open call options with the Covered Call and Option Debit Spread Strategies. Both of these strategies are limited risk strategies as the short calls are 'covered' by the ownership of the underlying stock or a call option with a lower strike price. The example below is a 'sell to open' order to sell short the Microsoft Mar 38-strike call option at the market. This would result in being short the call option.

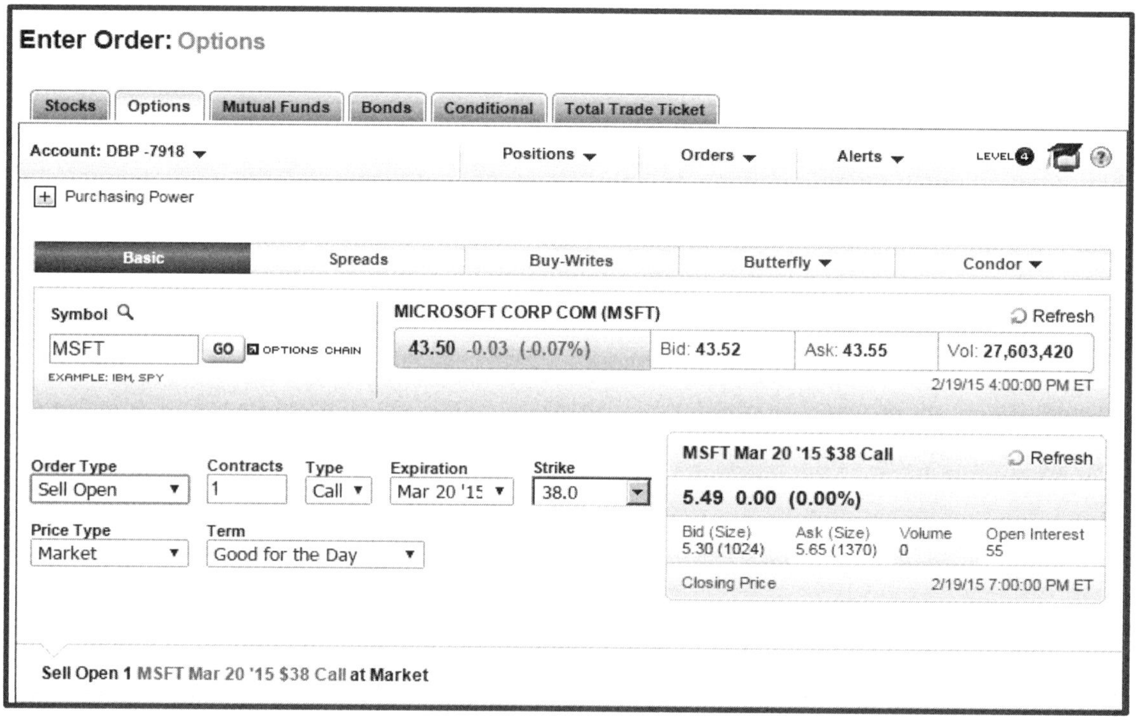

The example below is a 'buy to close' order to buy back the short Microsoft Mar 38-strike call option at the market. This would result in closing out the short call option.

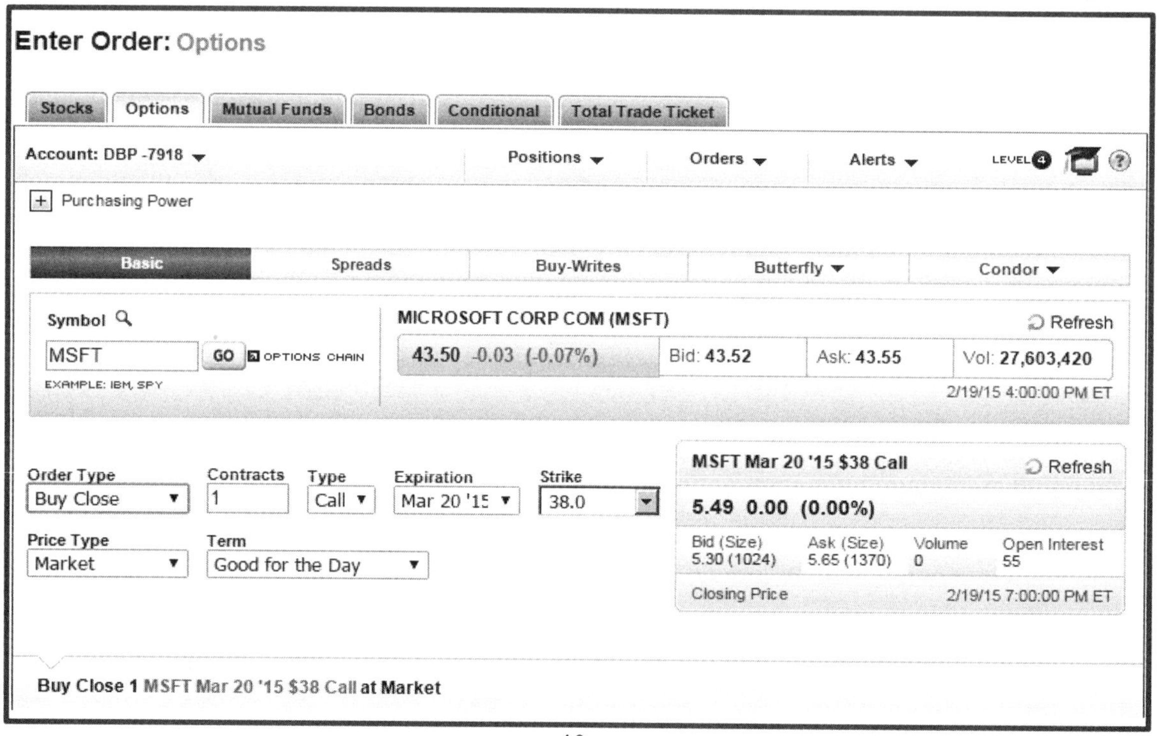

Option Pricing

Option premiums consist of intrinsic value and time value. At option expiration, options lose all time value and consist of only intrinsic value. Intrinsic value is the difference between the option strike price and the current price of the underlying stock. The intrinsic value of a call option is calculated by subtracting the strike price of the option from the current stock price. For example, let's assume Apple (AAPL) stock is currently trading at 75.00 and the April 70-Strike call option is priced at 7.00 points. The intrinsic value of this option would be 5.00 points.

Current Stock Price of 75.00 Minus Strike Price of 70.00 = 5.00 Intrinsic Value

The time value of an option is calculated by subtracting the intrinsic value from the total value of the option. In the above example the 70-Strike option priced at 7.00 would have 2.00 points of time value.

Option Price of 7.00 Minus Intrinsic Value of 5.00 = Time Value of 2.00

In the above example, if the Apple April 80-Strike call option is priced at 3.00 then this call option would have no intrinsic value and would only contain time value.

Current Stock Price of 75.00 Minus Strike Price of 80.00 = 0.00 Intrinsic Value

Option Price of 3.00 Minus Intrinsic Value of 0.00 = Time Value of 3.00

The intrinsic value of a put option is calculated by subtracting the current price of the stock from the strike price of the put. Let's assume again that Apple stock is trading at 75.00 and the AAPL April 80-Strike put option is priced at 8.00 points. The intrinsic value of this option would be 5.00 points and the time value would be 3.00 points.

Put Strike Price of 80.00 Minus Current Stock Price of 75.00 = 5.00 Intrinsic Value

Option Price of 8.00 Minus Intrinsic Value of 5.00 = Time Value of 3.00

In the above example, if the Apple April 70-Strike put option is priced at 2.00 then this put option would have no intrinsic value and would only contain time value.

Put Strike Price of 70.00 Minus Stock Price of 75.00 = 0.00 Intrinsic Value

Option Price of 2.00 Minus Intrinsic Value of 0.00 = Time Value of 2.00

How to Read Option Symbols

An option symbol is comprised of several components that define the underlying stock or ETF and information about the specific option contract. A weekly option symbol consists of the stock or ETF trading symbol, year of expiration, month of expiration, expiration date, option type (call or put) and strike-price.

There are many financial websites available today that will give you option quotes. I like to use Yahoo Finance or the Chicago Board Options Exchange website at www.cboe.com to obtain option quotes.

The symbol for the General Electric Jan 2017 25-Strike call option is GE170120C00025000. Let's look at the components of this option symbol.

GE, 17, 01, 20, C, 00025000

GE is the trading symbol for General Electric
17 is the expiration year 2017
01 is the expiration month of January
20 is the expiration date which is January 20th in this example
C designates a call option (put options are designated with a "P")
00025000 designates a 25-Strike price.

Exercise and Assignment

Exercise is the term used when the buyer of an option uses their right to purchase or sell the underlying stock at the strike price on the close of option expiration day (third Friday of expiration month). Assignment is the term used when the seller of an option is obligated to deliver or receive the underlying stock. When the option buyer exercises their option contract, the seller of the contract receives a notice of assignment from their broker. Your broker handles the entire option exercise/assignment transaction.

Most option contracts are never exercised. They either expire worthless or are closed out prior to option expiration. *All options that are 'in-the-money' at option expiration are automatically exercised.*

A Call Option Is 'In-the-Money' if the Strike Price Is Lower Than the Stock Price

A Put Option Is 'In-the-Money' if the Strike Price Is Higher Than the Stock Price

If you are long or short a put or a call and the option is in-the-money approaching option expiration you must close out your option position prior to the close on option expiration day or the option will be automatically be exercised/assigned.

LEAPS

LEAPS (Long-term Equity Anticipation Securities) are long term options with expiration dates that are up to three years away. Not all optionable stocks trade LEAPS options. LEAPS options can be used for long-term investing, hedging or to generate income.

'Feel the Power'

The information presented in this Chapter is sometimes difficult to understand especially for novice investors. The upcoming Chapters on option investing give detailed instructions on how to implement the option strategies along with actual trade examples. I think your understanding of option investing will become much clearer as you read these Chapters. Please refer back to this Chapter as needed when you read the upcoming Chapters on option investing.

Once you understand the mechanics of option investing you can take advantage of the tremendous profit opportunities available with option investing. I know the power of options. Last month my option investing produced a $202,288.77 monthly profit. Brokerage statements confirming this monthly profit are listed in Chapter 6.

We are now ready to move on to the *Small Cap Option Strategy* which is the first option strategy we will explore.

Chapter 6

Becoming a 'Shoestring Millionaire'

Getting a high return with a small investment is the secret to becoming what I call a 'Shoestring Millionaire'. The key to achieving a high return is to use leverage. You may recall from the Preface that stocks have historically provided an 11.6% average compounded rate of return over the long term. While this rate of return far exceeds the historical returns for home prices and fixed income investments, it would take many years to turn a small investment into a large investment with an 11.6% annual return. For example, it would take more than six years to double your investment with an 11.6% compounded rate of return.

'Good' and 'Bad' Leverage

In my experience the best way to achieve a high rate of investment return is to invest in options. Options give you the 'leverage' you need to generate a high rate of return with a small investment which can enable us to become a 'Shoestring Millionaire'. But I want to make an important distinction here. There is 'Good' leverage and there is 'Bad' leverage. The strategies presented in this book use 'Good' leverage. When you use 'Good' leverage you can't lose more money than you invest.

In this Chapter we will explore purchasing call options which can provide leverage that can enable you to realize a high rate of return over a short period of time. When you purchase a call option the most you can lose is the cost of the option regardless of the price movement of the underlying stock. Even if the price of a stock drops to zero and the stock is 'delisted' from the exchange the most you can lose is the cost you paid for the option. This would be an example of 'Good' leverage.

Purchasing options incurs limited risk which is different from Forex trading or trading futures contracts. I have seen a lot of advertisements lately touting the '100 to 1' or even '200 to 1' leverage available from Forex trading. While this kind of leverage can produce high returns it can be dangerous to your financial health. If you invest $10,000 in '200 to 1' leveraged contract a 10% adverse move can wipe out your $10,000 investment and trigger a $190,000 margin call that will force you to pay the brokerage firm an additional $190,000 to meet the margin call. Recently the Amaranth hedge fund 'blew up' as a result of margin calls the fund received on its energy futures contracts. These types of margin calls have occurred in the past and with the use of 'Bad' leverage will probably occur again in the future. More often than not the use of this type of leverage eventually ends badly for investors.

Options Can Provide a High Rate of Return With a Small Investment Which Would Allows Us to Become Shoestring Millionaires

Purchasing call options can provide the leverage that allows you to achieve a high return with a small investment. The table below contains actual call option prices for Merck (MRK). Merck stock is trading at 41.03. Let's focus on the MRK 40-Strike call option (circled). Purchasing this option would cost 1.10 points or $110 (plus commission) at the current trading price.

MRK **41.03 -0.06**

Calls	Last Sale	Bid	Ask	Open Int
06 Sep 30.00 (MRK IF)	11.10	10.90	11.10	231
06 Sep 32.50 (MRK IZ)	8.60	8.40	8.60	150
06 Sep 35.00 (MRK IG)	6.10	5.90	6.10	263
06 Sep 37.50 (MRK IU)	3.60	3.40	3.60	474
06 Sep 40.00 (MRK IH)	1.10	1.00	1.10	12,744

An ordinary investor would:

- **Buy Merck stock at 41.03**
- **Let's Assume Stock Increases 10% to 45.13**

Net Result:

- **Large Investment: $4,103**
- **Small Profit: 10%**

A "Shoestring Millionaire" would:

- **Buy MRK 40-Strike call at 1.10**
- **Let's Assume Stock Increases 10% to 45.13**

Net Result:

- **Small Investment: $110**
- **Large Profit: 366% ***

* Stock price of 45.13 Minus 40-Strike Price = Option Value of 5.13
5.13 Option Value Minus 1.10 Cost = 4.03 Option Profit
4.03 Profit Divided by 1.10 Cost = 366% Option Return

Let's assume we purchase 10 of the Merck 40-Strike call options previously mentioned. Our total investment would be $1,100 plus commission (10 X $110 option price = $1,100). And let's again assume that the price of Merck stock increases 10% from 41.03 to 45.13. The value of the 40-Strike call option would be 5.13 (stock price of 45.13 minus strike price of 40 = 5.13 option value). After subtracting the 1.10 cost of the option from the current 5.13 value results in a 4.03 profit or $403 per option. Our total profit for purchasing 10 options would be $4,030. When purchasing options our risk is limited to the purchase price of the option. In this example our total risk for purchasing ten options would be $1,100.

Big Gains Do Not Require Big Risks

In order for a stock investor to realize a $4,030 profit from a 10% move in Merck stock they would have to purchase 982 shares which would require a $40,291 investment. Which brings up the question . . . Would you rather risk $40,291 to make a $4,030 profit (buying stock) or risk $1,100 to make the same $4,030 profit (buying options)? Options trading allows you to make big gains that do not require big risks.

The Power of Leverage

Let's take this example one step further. Let's assume that you were able to make several of these trades consecutively. I know that losing trades are inevitable with any strategy and that every trade cannot be a big winner but for the sake of demonstration just bear with me for a moment. If you invested $1,100 and made a 366% return it would only take four such trades for your $1,100 investment to grow to $518,724 and after five trades your $1,100 investment grows to $2,417,253. Again, these results are strictly hypothetical but clearly demonstrate the power of leverage.

Trade Number	Starting Value	Percent Return	Profit	Ending Value
1	$1,100	366%	$4,026	$5,126
2	$5,126	366%	$18,761	$23,887
3	$23,887	366%	$87,427	$111,314
4	$111,314	366%	$407,410	$518,724
5	$518,724	366%	$1,898,530	$2,417,254
6	$2,417,254	366%	$8,847,149	$11,264,403
7	$11,264,403	366%	$41,227,716	$52,492,119

Options can provide spectacular returns without big risks . . . why doesn't everyone invest in them?

I think that in general options trading has been shrouded in mystery for the average investor. Most investors don't invest in options because they don't understand options and they have heard too many myths and misconceptions concerning options trading. When something is not understood, it is often feared. I believe this is the case with option trading. The biggest misconception related to option trading is that it is 'too risky'. But that is simply not true. In the previous example for Merck options we learned that a stock investor has to risk $40,291 to receive the same profit potential as the options investor who only risks $1,100. Trading stocks is more risky than trading options because more of your money is at risk. Option trading is also more versatile as you can profit in up, down or sideways markets.

While option trading provides huge profit potential, you can't win with trading options unless you fully understand how they work. Successful option trading also requires a reliable system that tells you when to buy and sell so that you don't wind up trading on 'hunches' and guesswork. The goal of this Chapter is to demonstrate in detail the risks and rewards associated with trading options. The most effective way to achieve our goal is to examine the risk/reward characteristics of several options trades.

We discovered in Chapter 4 that the *Small Cap Stock Strategy* uses trend lines to purchase small cap stocks and that the strategy has proven to be a powerful approach for selecting profitable stocks. Fourteen years of historical results using the *Small Cap Stock Strategy* rules show that the strategy has proven to be a reliable, profitable approach to stock selection during both bull and bear markets. Over a fourteen year period that included three bear markets the strategy produced an average 3,411% return with minimal risk for a broad sampling of small cap stocks in almost every industry. The *Small Cap Stock Strategy* rules generate clearly defined 'buy' and 'sell' signals. One of the best ways to implement the *Small Cap Stock Strategy* would be to purchase call options when a 'buy' signal is in effect. Let's review the rules for a strategy that purchases call options on small cap stocks that are in a closing price up trend.

Small Cap Option Strategy Rules

(Strategy # 2)

1. **Select a small cap stock**
2. **Purchase an 'In-the-Money'* call option on a small cap stock if its 40-Day Weighted Trend Line (WTL) is above the 80-Day WTL**
3. **Sell any call option if its underlying stock 40-Day WTL crosses below the 80-Day WTL**

* In-the-Money call options will be explained in detail later in this Chapter

Small Cap Option Strategy Example

This example is based on actual prices. Allscripts Healthcare Solutions (MRDX) is a small cap healthcare technology company with a market capitalization of 1.06 billion$. Allscripts qualifies as a small cap stock with a market cap of less than 2.37 billion$ which satisfies Rule # 1. Allscripts (MDRX) is trading at 22.28. The MDRX 40-Day Weighted Trend Line (WTL) is above the 80-Day WTL which satisfies Rule # 2. The MDRX October 20-Strike call option (circled below) is trading at 2.60. The strike price of the 20-Strike call option is below the current 22.28 price of MDRX stock so this would be an 'in-the-money' call option and would qualify for purchase under the *Small Cap Option Strategy* rules. If you decided to purchase this option place an online order or give your broker an order to buy 'to open' the MDRX October 20-Strike call option at the market.

If the Allscripts stock's 40-Day WTL crosses below the 80-Day WTL then sell the MDRX 20-Strike call option 'at the market'. If the 40-Day WTL remains above the 80-Day WTL then sell on option expiration day which in this example would be Friday October 20th. A Call Option Return Analysis for a MDRX call option will be covered later in this Chapter.

The Key to Profitable Option Trading

The preceding example for the Merck 40-Strike call option demonstrated the high profit potential available from buying call options. The key to profitable call option trading is to purchase call options on stocks that are increasing in price. The value of a call option will increase as the price of the underlying stock increases so selecting stocks that will move up in price is vital for successful call option trading. The *Small Cap Stock Strategy* buys small cap stocks that are in a price up trend. Using this strategy to select stocks for call option purchases gives us a tremendous advantage as we know in advance the most likely future price direction of a stock.

When you buy a call option, the value of the option increases 'dollar for dollar' as the price of the underlying stock moves above the strike price of the call option purchased. Let's look at an example of a call option purchase so that you can fully understand this important concept. The quote table below contains actual call option prices for Allscripts (MDRX) stock.

MDRX **22.28 +0.05**

Calls	Last Sale	Bid	Ask	Open Int
06 Oct 17.50 (MXQ JW)	0	4.60	5.00	0
06 Oct 20.00 (MXQ JD)	2.30	2.30	2.60	173
06 Oct 22.50 (MXQ JX)	0.55	0.70	0.90	554
06 Oct 25.00 (MXQ JE)	0.25	0.05	0.25	274

Option Profits are Directly Related to Stock Price Movement

The table below lists the value of the Allscripts (MDRX) 20-Strike call option at option expiration for various 'what if' prices for Allscripts stock. You can see that the value of the option is directly related to the price of Allscripts stock at expiration. If Allscripts stock closes at 24.00 then the 20-Strike option will be worth 4.00 points or $400 (stock price of 24.00 minus strike price of 20.0 = option value of 4.00). This represents a 54% profit on the 2.60 purchase price of the option. If Allscripts stock closes at 30.00 the value of the 20-Strike call option would be 10.00 which represents a 285% return on the 2.60 cost of the option.

Option value increases 'dollar for dollar' once the stock price moves above the strike price of the option purchased

Allscripts Call Option Increases in Value as the Price of Allscripts Stock Increases

Allscripts Stock Price at Option Expiration	24.00	26.00	28.00	30.00
Value of 20-Strike Call Option	4.00	6.00	8.00	10.00
Percent Return on 2.60 Cost	54%	131%	208%	285%

Now that we know that the price movement of the underlying stock determines the profitability of call option purchases, we can construct a profitable option strategy based on this important concept. If we can select stocks moving up in price then we can realize enormous profits by purchasing call options on such stocks. We also know that the *Small Cap Stock Strategy* has a long history of selecting stocks with the best price appreciation potential. Combining the rules of the *Small Cap Stock Strategy* for selecting stocks with a rule for purchasing an in-the-money call option results in a highly profitable option strategy based on the actual profit results that follow.

Option Quote

There are many financial websites available today that will give you option quotes. I like to use the Chicago Board Options Exchange website at www.cboe.com to obtain option quotes as it will give you comprehensive bid/ask option quotes that include all of the strike prices and expiration months for both put and call options. After logging on to the cboe.com home page click 'Quotes'. Then click 'Delayed Quotes'. Then type in the stock symbol and select 'List all options and LEAPS' and then click 'Submit'. This will give bid and ask quotes for all of the strike prices and expiration months available for that particular stock. The call option quotes are listed on the left side and put option quotes are listed on the right side.

The table below contains actual option quotes for Allscripts stock symbol MDRX. Let's focus on the Jan 22.50-Strike call option which is circled below. If we were purchasing this option we would expect to pay the 'ask' price of 2.05. Options normally cover 100 shares of stock. If we purchase one Jan 22.50-Strike call option at 2.05 we would pay \$205 plus commission (2.05 X 100). Option expiration day is normally the third Friday of the option expiration month. In this example, the January call option would expire on Friday January 19th or in about four months. The value of his call option on option expiration day would be determined by the price of the underlying Allscripts stock.

MDRX **22.28** **+0.05**

Calls	Last Sale	Bid	Ask	Open Int
07 Jan 15.00 (MXQ AC)	7.50	7.40	7.80	412
07 Jan 17.50 (MXQ AW)	5.20	5.00	5.50	777
07 Jan 20.00 (MXQ AD)	3.40	3.30	3.70	812
07 Jan 22.50 (MXQ AX)	1.60	1.85	2.05	650
07 Jan 25.00 (MXQ AE)	1.15	0.75	1.05	303

Allscripts stock is currently trading at 22.28 (circled). Purchasing the 22.50-Strike call option would be considered an 'out-of-the-money' option as the 22.50-Strike price is greater than the current price of 22.28 of the underlying stock. An out-of-the-money option consists of only time value in this example 2.05 points and has no intrinsic valve. If Allscripts stock closes at 22.50 or below at option expiration on January 19th then this option would expire worthless.

'Out-of-the-Money' Call Option Purchase Example

The value of a call option at option expiration is determined by the price of the underlying stock. The call option return table below displays the value of the 22.50-Strike call option assuming various prices of Allscripts stock at option expiration. The first row of the table is labeled '% Change' and assumes various percent changes in Allscripts stock at option expiration from a -10% decline to a +40% increase in price. The second row is labeled 'Stock Price' and is the Allscripts stock price that corresponds to the percentage change on the row above. The bottom row labeled 'Profit or Loss' lists the corresponding percentage change in the option value related to the price change in the stock.

This option would acquire intrinsic value if the price of Allscripts stock trades above 22.50. Let's say we are expecting a 10% price increase in Allscripts stock by option expiration. A 10% increase in the current 22.28 price would result in a 24.51 stock price (circled). If Allscripts stock closed at 24.51 at option expiration, the 22.50-Strike call option would acquire intrinsic value and would be worth 2.01 points (24.51 stock price minus 22.50-Strike price). The cost of the 22.50-Strike option was 2.05 and the option is now worth 2.01. This would result in a small .04 loss which translates to a 2.0% loss. This analysis reveals that purchasing this option with an expectation of a 10% stock price increase would not be worthwhile.

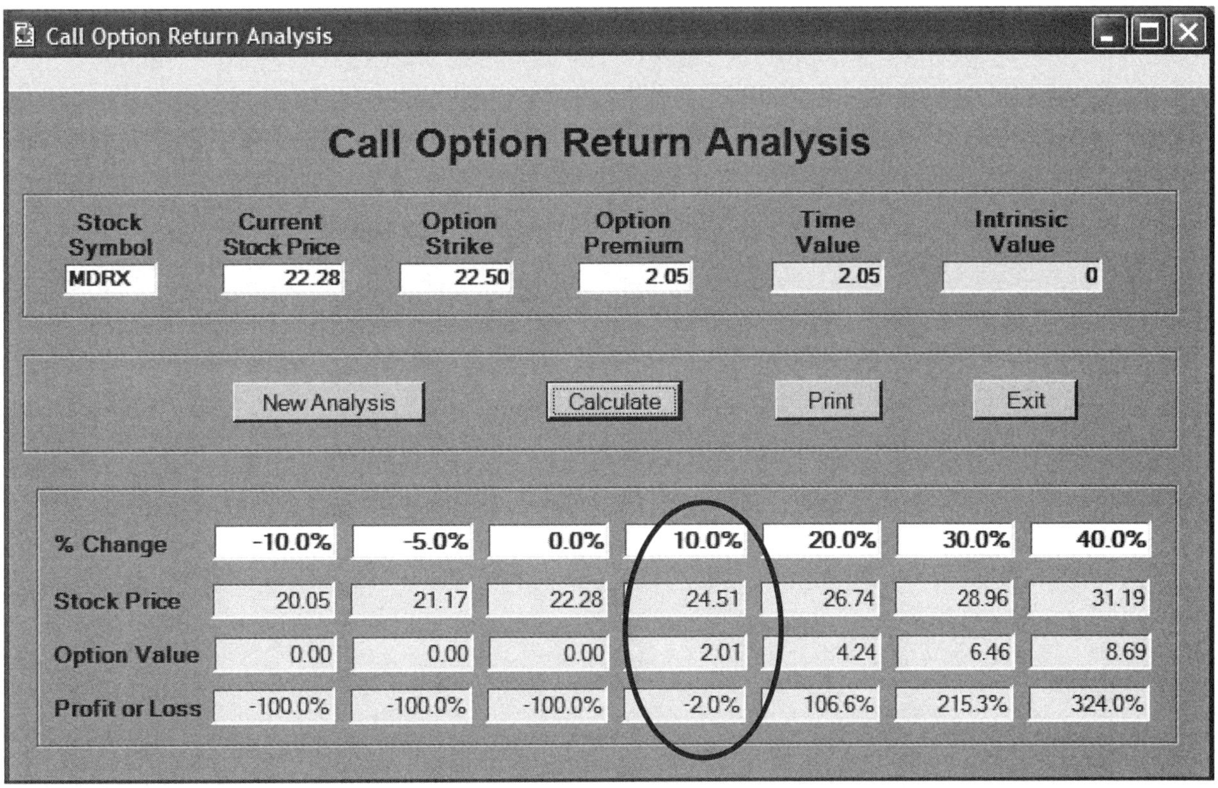

Stock Symbol	Current Stock Price	Option Strike	Option Premium	Time Value	Intrinsic Value
MDRX	22.28	22.50	2.05	2.05	0

% Change	-10.0%	-5.0%	0.0%	10.0%	20.0%	30.0%	40.0%
Stock Price	20.05	21.17	22.28	24.51	26.74	28.96	31.19
Option Value	0.00	0.00	0.00	2.01	4.24	6.46	8.69
Profit or Loss	-100.0%	-100.0%	-100.0%	-2.0%	106.6%	215.3%	324.0%

If Allscripts stock closed at 22.50 or lower at option expiration then the 22.50-Strike option would expire worthless and would result in a total loss of the 2.05 cost of the option. If there is no change in Allscripts stock and it closes at 22.28 at option expiration the above analysis reveals that 22.50-Strike call option would have no intrinsic value and would expire worthless.

A 10% Stock Increase Results in an Option Loss

The preceding call option return table reveals that the purchase of the 22.50-Strike out-of-the-money call option requires more than a 10% increase in the price of Allscripts stock just to break even. In general, purchasing 'out-of-the-money' call options requires a large stock price increase in order to be profitable.

Out-of-the-Money Call Options Consist of 100% Time Value
Options Lose All of their Time Value at Expiration
This Requires a Large Stock Price Increase for the Option to Be Profitable

Let's next examine purchasing an 'in-the-money' call option. Remember that when you purchase an option you can sell it at any time prior to option expiration day. If you sell prior to option expiration the price you receive for the sale of the option would depend on the current price of the underlying stock.

'In-the-Money' Call Option Example

The table below displays the profit potential for purchasing the Allscripts 17.50-Strike 'in-the-money' call option (circled in the previous option quote table).

Note: The Call Option Return Analysis tables presented in this Chapter are not required to implement the Small Cap Stock Option Strategy. The tables are presented here to help compare the returns of 'out-of-the-money' call options versus 'in-the-money' calls.

Call Option Return Analysis

Call Option Return Analysis

Stock Symbol	Current Stock Price	Option Strike	Option Premium	Time Value	Intrinsic Value
MDRX	22.28	17.50	5.50	0.72	4.78

New Analysis | Calculate | Print | Exit

% Change	-10.0%	-5.0%	0.0%	10.0%	20.0%	30.0%	40.0%
Stock Price	20.05	21.17	22.28	24.51	26.74	28.96	31.19
Option Value	2.55	3.67	4.78	7.01	9.24	11.46	13.69
Profit or Loss	-53.6%	-33.3%	-13.1%	27.4%	67.9%	108.4%	148.9%

'In-the-Money' Call Option Trade Example

Left Hand Column – Stock Price Decrease (Circled)

% Change: -10.0% --- This assumes a 10% decline in the price of MDRX stock
Stock Price: 20.05 --- The MDRX stock price after a 10% decline
Option Value: 2.55 --- The value of the 17.50-Strike call option assuming a MDRX stock price of 20.05 at option expiration
Profit or Loss: -53.6% --- Percent loss of current option value of 2.55 from original purchase price of 5.50

Right Hand Column – Stock Price Increase (Circled)

% Change: 40.0% --- This assumes a 40% increase in the price of MDRX stock
Stock Price: 31.19 --- The MDRX stock price after a 40% increase
Option Value: 13.69 --- The value of the 17.50-Strike call option assuming a MDRX stock price of 31.19 at option expiration
Profit or Loss: 148.9% --- Percent profit of current option value of 13.69 from original purchase price of 5.50

In-the-Money Options Incur Less Risk

We can see from the preceding return analysis table that the MDRX 17.50-Strike 'in-the-money' call option purchase will produce substantial profits with a moderate 10 to 30% stock price increase. This 'in-the-money' option only has .72 points of time value. Allscripts stock would only have to increase .72 points in price to 23.00 by option expiration for this trade to break even and start producing profits. A flat stock price (no change) at option expiration would result in a -13.1% loss. Compare this to an 'out-of-the-money' call option purchase which would result in a total loss of your investment with a flat stock price. This sample trade clearly demonstrates that investing in 'in-the-money' call options can reduce the overall risk of option investing. This 'in-the-money' call option purchase strikes a good balance between reward and risk compared to a higher risk 'out-of-the-money' call option purchase.

The MDRX 'in-the-money' return analysis table reveals that a +20% to +40% increase in stock price results in a lower return when compared to the 'out-of-the-money' option example. But for the stock price changes from +10% to -10% the 'in-the-money' option produces a higher return than the 'out-of-the-money'. The +10% stock price increase results in a 27.4% profit on the 'in-the-money' option versus a -2.0% *loss* for the 'out-of-the-money' option and the unchanged stock price results in a 13.1% loss for the 'in-the-money' versus a 100% loss for the 'out-of-the-money' option.

At option expiration an option loses all time value and is comprised of only intrinsic value. An 'in-the-money' call option is comprised of both time value and intrinsic value. The deeper an option is 'in-the-money' the more intrinsic value it will have. In this example the MDRX 'in-the-money' option premium is comprised of 13% time value and 87% intrinsic value. An 'in-the-money' option does not require a large upward price move in the underlying stock to break even or to produce a profit.

Of course, 'out-of-the-money' options will produce a higher percentage return than 'in-the-money' options if there is a substantial price increase in the underlying stock. But remember that when you invest in options you must be correct not only about the future price movement of the underlying stock but you must also be correct about the time frame during which this movement must occur (before option expiration). You must plan on the possibility that you are not correct about the price movement and/or time frame. If you are wrong about the price direction or time frame you could lose your whole investment with an 'out-of-the-money' option. This is not an acceptable risk if you want to 'stay in the game' after unanticipated market corrections or price declines.

Trade Off

After many years of trying to 'Hit a Home Run' by investing in 'out-of-the-money' options I realized that this type of strategy was too risky as I had too many 'out-of-the-money' options expire worthless. No matter how good your stock selection is, there will be periods when you are wrong and cannot afford to risk your options expiring worthless.

"The key to making money in stocks is not to get scared out of them."

Peter Lynch

Every trader has a different risk tolerance and must decide if they want to trade 'in-the-money' call options with lower risk and a smaller profit potential or 'out-of-the-money' calls with higher risk but also with greater profit potential. Purchasing an 'out-of-the-money' call option requires a substantial price increase in the underlying stock price in order to be profitable and incurs considerably more risk than an 'in-the-money' option. A flat or slightly down price movement in the underlying stock at option expiration can result in a total loss of your investment for an 'out-of-the-money' option. 'Out-of-the-money' call purchases will provide much higher returns, however, if there is a substantial price increase in the underlying stock.

Advantages of 'In-the-Money' Call Purchases versus 'Out-of-the-Money'

- 'In-the-Money' calls contain less time value and more intrinsic value
- Does not require large stock price increase to breakeven or profit
- Fewer 'total losses' of investment
- Less overall risk
- Higher percentage of winning trades

Disadvantages of 'In-the-Money' Call Purchases versus 'Out-of-the-Money'

- 'In-the-Money' calls have a higher premium cost which requires a bigger investment
- 'In-the-Money' calls realize lower returns if the underlying stock experiences a substantial price increase

The Four 'Keys' to Profitable Option Investing

My experience has shown that the four most important factors necessary for profitable option investing are:

1) Purchasing In-the-Money Options

2) Diversification

3) Stock selection

4) Using a rule based strategy with a history of profitable performance

Purchasing In-The-Money Options

The previous example for the Allscripts 'in-the-money' call option purchase clearly demonstrates that purchasing 'in-the-money' calls has a much better risk/reward profile than purchasing 'out-of-the-money options'. Purchasing 'out-of-the-money' call options requires a large upward move in the price of the underlying stock in order to be profitable. If you are wrong about the timing of this required price movement or if the stock price is flat or slightly down at option expiration you could lose 100% of your investment. This is not an acceptable risk. No matter how good your stock selection is, there will be periods when you are wrong and cannot afford to risk a total loss of your investment. Investing in 'in-the-money' options with ample intrinsic value increases the probability of success in option investing.

Diversification

Diversification is an important part of profitable options investing. This is especially true when investing in individual stock options versus an index option on a broad based index such as the S&P 500 Index. A major advantage of option purchases is 'truncated risk', whereby your loss is limited to the premium paid for the option yet your profit potential is not limited. A diversified portfolio will allow you to take full advantage of truncated risk. While some of your option positions may lose value or expire worthless, a profitable trade can offset several unprofitable trades. A diversified options portfolio can produce a positive return even if most of the options in the portfolio are losers.

Stock Selection

Stock selection is important because the intrinsic value of an option is determined by the price movement of the underlying stock. As we discovered in this Chapter, options lose all time value at expiration and only contain intrinsic value which is determined by the price of the underlying stock. When purchasing a call option you obviously want to purchase an option on a stock with good price appreciation potential as the intrinsic value of a call option increases 'dollar for dollar' as the price of the underlying stock moves above the strike price of a call option.

Rule Based Strategy

Using a rule based strategy to make buy and sell decisions can give you the confidence and discipline necessary to be a successful options trader. Historical and actual profit performance results presented in this book demonstrate that the *Small Cap Stock Strategy* is an excellent way to discover stocks with the best price appreciation potential which can give you the edge in option trading.

Four Advantages of Options Trading

1. ***Size Doesn't Matter***

   Options can be traded in almost any size account. This allows traders with small trading accounts to take part in this opportunity. Options can be purchased for as little as a few hundred dollars and a diversified options portfolio can be established with just a few thousand dollars.

2. ***Risk Is Limited***

   Risk is limited to the purchase price of the call option regardless of how far the underlying stock may fall in price. With option purchases you are not required to add funds to your account with adverse market moves and there is no threat of margin calls.

3. ***High Leverage***

   Options provide substantially more leverage than stocks and mutual funds. A 10% price increase in a stock can easily produce a 50% return for the related call option.

4. ***Profit Potential Is Not Limited***

   Most importantly option profit potential is not limited. When you purchase a call option, the value of the option increases 'dollar for dollar' as the price of the underlying stock moves above the strike price of the call option purchased.

Small Cap Option Strategy Contributes to Recent $202,288.77 Monthly Profit

The *Small Cap Option Strategy* contributed to a $202,288.77 profit over a recent one month period from October 28th through November 25th. My BrownCo statement below shows a monthly profit of $122,361.50 and the E*Trade account statement that follows shows a $79,927.27 profit over the same period bringing the total monthly profits to $202,288.77.

Note: These are large trading accounts in which I trade multiple contracts (as many as 24 contracts per option). Trading one contract per option would require a considerably smaller brokerage account.

BROWN|CO

ONE BEACON STREET, BOSTON, MA 02108-3102

Page: 1 of 14

Account Number:

Your Monthly Brokerage Account Statement | October 28, 2005 - November 25, 2005

Telephone: (800) 965-1190

Portfolio Summary

	Market Value on 10/28/05	Market Value on 11/25/05	Unrealized Gain/Loss	% of Portfolio
Cash/Margin	53,423.41	14,354.17		4
Money Balance	**$53,423.41**	**$14,354.17**		**4**
Long Options	206,050.00	348,040.00	122,361.50	96
Equities and Options	**$206,050.00**	**$348,040.00**	**$122,361.50**	**96**
Total Account Value *	**$259,473.41**	**$362,394.17**	**$122,361.50**	**100**

E*TRADE FINANCIAL QUOTES GO | SEARCH GO Help Center | Open an Account LOG OFF

Accounts | Trading & Portfolios | Quotes & Research | Mutual Funds & ETFs | Retirement & Planning | Banking & Credit Cards | Mortgages & Home Equity

Trade Portfolios View Orders | Balances | Transaction History | Account Records | Power E*TRADE

November 25, 2005 2:54 PM ET

Portfolios

Alerts | Transfer Money | Bill Pay | Help

Portfolios | Performance & Value | Positions | NEW! Gains & Losses

Account/Watch List: LEGACY PUBLISHING LLC Create / Edit List View: Performance Customize

Market Value: $374,901.34 ($79,927.27 / 27.10%) DJIA 10,931.62 ▲ +15.53 Nasdaq 2,263.01 ▲ +3.03

REFRESH | LAUNCH MARKETCASTER | EXPORT TO EXCEL

Symbol		Current Price	Change $	Change %	Day's Gain	Qty	Price Paid	Total Gain $	Total Gain %	Market Val	Edit
AAQDH	Trade	28.10	0.00	0.00%	$0.00	8	$20.10	$6,374.02	39.58%	$22,480.00	Edit
AXDH	Trade	20.60	0.00	0.00%	$0.00	15	$11.87	$13,058.78	73.19%	$30,900.00	Edit
AXDJ	Trade	11.20	0.00	0.00%	$0.00	4	$14.00	-$1,132.99	-20.19%	$4,480.00	Edit
CAMEM	Trade	17.30	0.00	0.00%	$0.00	3	$17.30	-$12.24	-0.24%	$5,190.00	Edit
CMJCV	Trade	99.60	16.60	20.00%	$4,980.00	3	$79.40	$6,027.78	25.27%	$29,880.00	Edit
DWNCP	Trade	19.60	-1.50	-7.11%	-$900.00	6	$20.65	-$654.48	-5.27%	$11,760.00	Edit
EJOED	Trade	6.60	0.00	0.00%	$0.00	6	$6.60	-$14.49	-0.36%	$3,960.00	Edit
GBZDN	Trade	42.30	0.00	0.00%	$0.00	2	$31.70	$2,098.52	32.99%	$8,460.00	Edit
GBZDP	Trade	35.40	0.00	0.00%	$0.00	1	$35.80	-$50.74	-1.41%	$3,540.00	Edit
GGDCD	Trade	115.50	6.50	5.96%	$1,300.00	2	$70.50	$8,978.52	63.58%	$23,100.00	Edit

E*TRADE FINANCIAL

QUOTES GO | SEARCH GO Help Center | Open an Account LOG OFF

Accounts | Trading & Portfolios | Quotes & Research | Mutual Funds & ETFs | Retirement & Planning | Banking & Credit Cards | Mortgages & Home Equity

Trade Portfolios View Orders | Balances | Transaction History | Account Records | Power E*TRADE

November 25, 2005 2:54 PM ET

Portfolios

Alerts | Transfer Money | Bill Pay | Help

Portfolios | Performance & Value | Positions | NEW! Gains & Losses

Account/Watch List: LEGACY PUBLISHING LLC Create / Edit List **View:** Performance Customize

Market Value: $374,901.34 ($79,927.27 / 27.10%) **DJIA** 10,931.62 ▲ +15.53 **Nasdaq** 2,263.01 ▲ +3.03

REFRESH | LAUNCH MARKETCASTER | EXPORT TO EXCEL

Symbol		Current Price	Change $	Change %	Day's Gain	Qty	Price Paid	Total Gain $	Total Gain %	Market Val	Edit
⊞ GGDCH	Trade	**98.20**	5.80	6.28%	$1,160.00	2	$79.00	$3,818.52	24.14%	$19,640.00	Edit
⊞ ITGDE	Trade	**12.40**	0.00	0.00%	$0.00	24	$9.25	$7,502.04	33.70%	$29,760.00	Edit
⊞ LESDB	Trade	**25.50**	-0.20	-0.78%	-$120.00	6	$23.47	$1,185.53	8.40%	$15,300.00	Edit
LTRCP	Trade	**18.90**	0.00	0.00%	$0.00	3	$18.90	-$12.24	-0.22%	$5,670.00	Edit
⊞ NQDCE	Trade	**20.10**	3.00	17.54%	$6,900.00	23	$9.3478	$24,662.80	114.35%	$46,230.00	Edit
NQDCF	Trade	**15.50**	1.70	12.32%	$850.00	5	$12.40	$1,536.26	24.72%	$7,750.00	Edit
⊞ PRUCM	Trade	**13.60**	0.00	0.00%	$0.00	12	$11.73	$2,201.03	15.59%	$16,320.00	Edit
QAADI	Trade	**25.30**	1.50	6.30%	$600.00	4	$17.80	$2,987.01	41.88%	$10,120.00	Edit
QAADJ	Trade	**20.60**	1.40	7.29%	$560.00	4	$18.10	$987.01	13.61%	$8,240.00	Edit
⊞ TIECI	Trade	**16.00**	0.20	1.27%	$160.00	8	$16.60	-$505.98	-3.80%	$12,800.00	Edit
⊞ UHBCJ	Trade	**11.30**	-0.40	-3.42%	-$800.00	20	$10.40	$1,745.04	8.37%	$22,600.00	Edit
⊞ XBADU	Trade	**10.70**	0.00	0.00%	$0.00	12	$10.60	$81.03	0.64%	$12,840.00	Edit
XTQEL	Trade	**22.70**	0.00	0.00%	$0.00	3	$23.80	-$342.24	-4.79%	$6,810.00	Edit
⊞ YHQDG	Trade	**8.60**	-0.50	-5.49%	-$750.00	15	$8.9667	-$591.22	-4.38%	$12,900.00	Edit
Cash					4,171.34					$4,171.34	
				Totals	$13,940.00		$294,974.07	$79,927.27	27.10%	$374,901.34	

LEGEND: ⊞ **collapsed** (click to expand) ⊟ **expanded** (click to collapse)

20-Minute Delayed quotes

Chapter 7

Buy Write Strategy

The *Shoestring Millionaire Buy Write Strategy* is a strategy designed to generate income from selling call option premium. A 'buy write' is established by buying a stock and 'writing' or selling its related call option. Normally one call option is sold for each 100 shares of stock that is purchased. A buy write is also known as a 'covered call' and implementing a covered call trade is also known as 'writing a covered call'.

There are two main objectives with the buy write strategy:

1) Generate income from the sale of a call options
2) Provide downside protection in the event your stock declines in price

The sale of a call option generates cash income in your brokerage account. One call option contract normally controls one hundred shares of the underlying stock. When you sell a call option cash is credited to your brokerage account. For example, if you sell a call option for 5.00 points, $500 will be credited to your account ($5.00 x 100 shares = $500). When you buy a stock and sell a call option the cash received from the sale of the call reduces the cost basis of your stock. This provides some downside protection in the event the stock declines in price.

The goal of the buy write strategy is to sell a call option on a stock that closes at or above the strike price of the short call option at option expiration. This results in the full profit potential of the buy write trade being realized and allows the call seller to 'pocket' the premium received for selling the call option. So selecting a stock that will close at or above the strike price of the short call is obviously important to the buy write trader. We learned in Chapter 2 that one of the best ways to select bullish stocks is to limit our stock selection to stocks that are in a closing price uptrend. In my experience this stock screening process is helpful for selecting stocks that would be good candidates for buy write investing.

Limited Profits and Limited Downside Protection

The profit potential of a buy write trade is limited to the income received for the sale of the call option. Downside protection for a decline in the stock price is also limited to the income received for the sale of the call option.

At option expiration there are two possible outcomes for a buy write trade:

1) The stock closes at or above the strike price of the short call option
2) The stock closes below the strike price of the short call option

If the underlying stock closes at or above the strike price of the short call option then the stock will be 'called'. The shares in your account will be sold at the strike price of the call option. This transaction is automatically handled by your broker on the Saturday following option expiration day. For example, let's assume you buy 100 shares of Unitedhealth (UNH) at 49.00 and sell one October 50-Strike call option at 5.00 points which expires on Friday October 21st. If UNH closes at 52.00 on option expiration day, your stock will be 'called' and your 100 shares of UNH will be sold at 50.00. You would receive a $5,000 credit in your brokerage account for the sale of the 100 shares. This transaction is automatic and occurs the next day Saturday October 22nd. You would keep the $500 option premium received for selling the 50-Strike call.

In this example if UNH closes at 48.00 at option expiration then the 50-Strike call option would expire worthless and you keep the $500 option premium received for selling the 50-Strike call. Your 100 shares of UNH would not be called and would remain in your brokerage account. You could then sell another UNH call option and establish a new buy write trade.

Buy Write Strategy Rules

(Strategy # 3)

1. **Purchase a stock if its 40-Day Weighted Trend Line (WTL) is above the 80-Day WTL**
2. **Sell the related call option**

Example

Let's examine a buy write trade I made recently to illustrate the strategy rules. The Google (GOOG) stock 40-Day Weighted Trend Line (WTL) is above its 80-Day WTL. On September 19th I purchased 100 shares of Google (GOOG) at 303.66 and sold the GOOG October 320-Strike call option for 6.30 points (see brokerage confirmations below). This was a one month trade.

09/19/05	Sell	-1	GGD-JD - CALL GOOGLE INC CL A $320 EXP 10/22/05 (As Of 09/19/05)	6.3000	**$618.72CR**
09/19/05	Buy	100	GOOG - GOOGLE INC CL A (As Of 09/19/05)	303.6580	**$30,377.75**

Buy Write Profit Potential

The trade analysis below displays the profit/loss potential assuming various prices of Google stock at option expiration for the Google trade I took recently.

Note: The Buy Write Analysis tables presented in this Chapter are not required to implement the Buy Write Strategy. The tables are presented here to help illustrate the potential returns and risks of buy write trades.

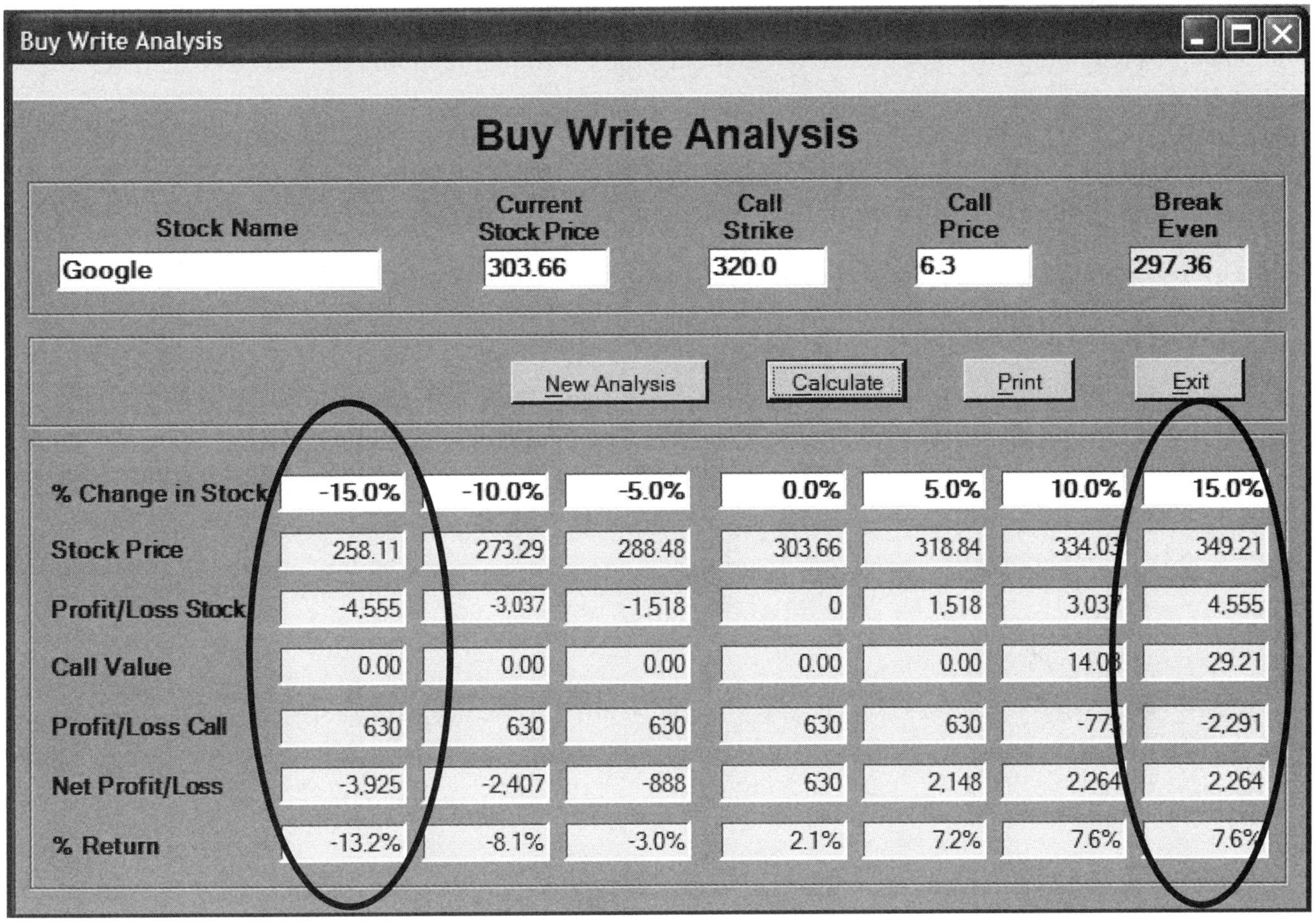

Stock Name	Current Stock Price	Call Strike	Call Price	Break Even
Google	303.66	320.0	6.3	297.36

% Change in Stock	-15.0%	-10.0%	-5.0%	0.0%	5.0%	10.0%	15.0%
Stock Price	258.11	273.29	288.48	303.66	318.84	334.03	349.21
Profit/Loss Stock	-4,555	-3,037	-1,518	0	1,518	3,037	4,555
Call Value	0.00	0.00	0.00	0.00	0.00	14.03	29.21
Profit/Loss Call	630	630	630	630	630	-773	-2,291
Net Profit/Loss	-3,925	-2,407	-888	630	2,148	2,264	2,264
% Return	-13.2%	-8.1%	-3.0%	2.1%	7.2%	7.6%	7.6%

Google Buy Write Trade Analysis

Left Hand Column – Stock Price Decline (Circled)

Stock % Change: -15% --- This assumes a 15% decline in the price of GOOG stock at option expiration
Stock Price: 258.11 --- The GOOG stock price after a 15% decline
Profit/Loss Stock: -4,555 --- The 100 shares of GOOG stock would realize a $4,555 loss if GOOG closes at 258.11 at option expiration
Call Value: 0 --- The GOOG 320-Strike call option would expire worthless if GOOG stock closes at 258.11 at option expiration
Profit/Loss Call: 630 --- The short 320-Strike call option produces a $630 profit if it expires worthless (sell call at 6.30 minus current value of 0 = +$630)
Net Profit/Loss: -3,925 --- Combining the stock loss of $4,555 with the $630 profit from the call option results in an overall net loss of $3,925 for this buy write trade
Spread % Return: -13.2% --- The $3,925 loss represents a -13.2% return on the $29,736 investment required to establish the buy write ($30,366 stock cost minus $630 credit for call option sale = $29,736 net cost)

Right Hand Column – Stock Price Increase (Circled)

Stock % Change: 15% --- This assumes a 15% increase in the price of GOOG stock at option expiration
Stock Price: 349.21 --- GOOG stock price after a 15% increase
Profit/Loss Stock: 4,555 --- The 100 shares of GOOG stock would realize a $4,555 profit if GOOG closes at 349.21 at option expiration
Call Value: 29.21 --- The GOOG 320-Strike call option would have a 29.21 value if GOOG stock closes at 349.21 at option expiration
Profit/Loss Call: -2,291 --- The short 320-Strike call option produces a $2,291 loss with a 29.21 value (sell at 6.30 minus current value of 29.21 = 22.91 loss or a $2,291 dollar loss)
Net Profit/Loss: 2,264 --- Combining the stock profit of $4,555 with the $2,291 loss from the call option results in an overall net profit of $2,264 for this buy write trade
Spread % Return: 7.6% --- The $2,264 profit represents a 7.6% return on the $29,736 investment required to establish the buy write ($30,366 stock cost minus $630 credit for call option sale = $29,736 net cost)

7.6% Monthly Return

We can see from the preceding analysis table that this covered call trade provides limited profits and limited downside protection in the event Google stock declines in price. If Google stock closes at or above the 320-Strike price at option expiration, then the full profit potential of $2,264 will be realized and the 100 shares of Google stock will be 'called'. If Google stock closes substantially higher than 320.0 at option expiration then the profit would still be limited to $2,264 which equates to a 7.6% return over the one month duration of this trade. I consider a 7.6% return a good return for a one month period especially if you 'rollover' this trade and repeat it every month. Google closed at 339.90 at option expiration on October 21st and the 100 shares of GOOG stock was called. The brokerage confirmations below show the call assignment at 320.00. One hundred shares of Google stock were called from my account at $320 per share and $32,000 was credited to the account.

Note: I wrote another Google covered call at the 320-Strike price so the confirmations below reflect the assignment of 200 shares of Google at 320.00 and $63,982.37 being credited to the brokerage account after the assignment commission of $17.63.

I included some more examples of covered call trades I made recently on the next page. We will then examine a long-term covered call trade using LEAPS options next.

10/24/05	Sell	-200	GOOG - GOOGLE INC CL A (As Of 10/21/05)	320.0000	$63,982.37CR

10/24/05	Assignment	10	DUZ-JC - CALL VIROPHARMA INC $15 EXP 10/22/05 (As Of 10/22/05)		
10/24/05	Assignment	5	XTQ-JL - CALL EXPRESS SCRIPTS $60 EXP 10/22/05 ****LONG TERM OPTION**** (As Of 10/22/05)		
10/24/05	Assignment	2	GGD-JD - CALL GOOGLE INC CL A $320 EXP 10/22/05 (As Of 10/22/05)		
10/24/05	Assignment	1	GGD-JT - CALL GOOGLE INC CL A $300 EXP 10/22/05 (As Of 10/22/05)		

Buy Write Income Results

I received $32,145.81 in income over the past five weeks from buy write trades. The table below lists the cash received in my brokerage accounts from selling call options (after commissions). Brokerage confirmations for these trades are listed in the Appendix.

Stock	Trade Date	Cash Credit		Stock	Trade Date	Cash Credit
Cigna Corp	31-Aug	$824.96		Chesapeake	28-Sep	$739.96
Allscripts	26-Aug	$700.96		Altria	8-Sep	$547.47
Biotech HLDRs	22-Aug	$404.98		Suncor Energy	16-Sep	$567.47
Tenaris	16-Sep	$704.96		Lone Star Tech	16-Sep	$427.48
Fording	27-Sep	$1,464.93		Nexen Inc	16-Sep	$586.22
Peabody	27-Sep	$1,044.95		Altria	16-Sep	$307.48
Joy Global	13-Sep	$744.96		Suncor Energy	16-Sep	$537.47
Valero Energy	13-Sep	$414.98		Chesapeake	21-Sep	$484.97
Encana	19-Sep	$539.97		Fording	9-Sep	$538.72
Marvel Tech	23-Aug	$539.97		Edison Int'l	6-Sep	$571.22
Allscripts	26-Aug	$1,017.95		Nexen Inc	14-Sep	$451.23
Cerner Corp	19-Sep	$599.97		National Oilwell	14-Sep	$537.47
Humana	26-Sep	$644.97		Meridian	23-Aug	$929.45
Tenaris	26-Sep	$1,184.94		National Oilwell	23-Aug	$739.71
Encana	23-Sep	$719.96		Viropharma	23-Aug	$1,812.42
Joy Global	19-Sep	$509.97		Tenaris	29-Aug	$476.47
Encana	20-Sep	$494.97		Florida Rock	26-Sep	$475.22
Encana	20-Sep	$539.97		Florida Rock	26-Sep	$496.22
Peabody	20-Sep	$444.98		Florida Rock	26-Sep	$541.22
Peabody	20-Sep	$479.97		Viropharma	30-Aug	$596.22
Cerner Corp	14-Sep	$624.97		Fording	30-Aug	$1,474.68
Google	20-Sep	$778.71		Transocean	30-Sep	$576.47
Allscripts	7-Sep	$471.22		National Oilwell	26-Aug	$486.47
Wellpoint	7-Sep	$772.96		Meridian	26-Aug	$572.97
				Totals		$32,145.81

Long Term Buy Writes

In Chapter 5 we learned that LEAPS (Long-Term Equity AnticiPation Securities) options are long-term options with a one to three year life span. Long term buy write trades can be implemented with the use of LEAPS call options. LEAPS options contain very rich premiums. These rich premiums are advantageous to option sellers. Selling LEAPS call options to establish buy write trades provides substantially higher profits and increased downside protection compared to short-term buy writes.

A 50 to 60% Return Potential

Long-term buy writes can realistically provide a 50 to 60% return with good downside protection if you sell an 'out-of-the-money' call option to establish the trade. Selling an 'in-the-money' call option can provide 40 to 50% downside protection depending on the strike price of the call option sold.

When you establish a short-term buy write trade you have to be 'right' about the short term price movement of a stock. You are anticipating that over the short-term the underlying stock will close at or above the strike price of the call option at option expiration. The timing of your entry for a short-term buy write can be very important. If you enter a buy write trade and the underlying stock subsequently declines in price there may not be enough time for the stock price to recover prior to option expiration. This could result in a loss.

The timing of 'when to enter' a LEAPS buy write trade is not as critical as entering a buy write trade with a short-term option expiration. LEAPS buy write trades provide substantial downside protection compared to short-term buy write trades. If you enter a LEAPS buy write trade and the underlying stock subsequently declines in price you have one to three years for the stock price to recover prior to option expiration.

Let's look at some examples of LEAPS buy write trades using actual stock and option prices. The CBOE option price table below contains the January '08 LEAPS call option prices for Apple (AAPL) stock. These options expire in about 25 months. A Buy Write Analysis was calculated using these actual put prices and is included on the next page.

AAPL					74.08 +0.13		
Calls	Bid	Ask	Open Int	Puts	Bid	Ask	Open Int
08 Jan 75.00 (WAA AO-E)	20.10	20.40	2098	08 Jan 75.00 (WAA MO-E)	14.90	15.20	559
08 Jan 80.00 (WAA AP-E)	18.10	18.40	1372	08 Jan 80.00 (WAA MP-E)	17.70	18.00	213
08 Jan 85.00 (WAA AQ-E)	16.30	16.70	121	08 Jan 85.00 (WAA MQ-E)	20.70	21.00	4
08 Jan 90.00 (WAA AR-E)	14.70	15.00	1130	08 Jan 90.00 (WAA MR-E)	23.90	24.30	190

A 51.6% Return

The Apple Buy Write Analysis below reveals that selling the AAPL 90-Strike LEAPS call option provides substantial profits and downside protection. If AAPL stock closes at or above 90.0 at option expiration in January a $3,062 profit would be realized (before commission) which translates to a 51.6% return.

Profits if Apple Stock Declines in Price

This trade also provides good downside protection in the event Apple stock declines in price. A 15% decline in the price of Apple stock at option expiration would result in a positive 6% return. A 5% decline in the price of Apple stock would result in a +18.5% return (before commission).

We will look at another example of a long-term buy write trade for Google next.

Note: Some of the stocks used as examples in this Chapter may have a stock split after this book is printed and their prices should be adjusted accordingly.

Buy Write Analysis

Buy Write Analysis

Stock Name	Current Stock Price	Call Strike	Call Price	Break Even
Apple	74.08	90	14.7	59.38

New Analysis | Calculate | Print | Exit

% Change in Stock	-15.0%	-10.0%	-6.0%	0.0%	20.0%	40.0%	60.0%
Stock Price	62.97	66.67	69.64	74.08	88.90	103.71	118.53
Profit/Loss Stock	-1,111	-741	-444	0	1,482	2,963	4,445
Call Value	0.00	0.00	0.00	0.00	0.00	13.71	28.53
Profit/Loss Call	1,470	1,470	1,470	1,470	1,470	99	-1,383
Net Profit/Loss	359	729	1,026	1,470	2,952	3,062	3,062
% Return	6.0%	12.3%	17.3%	24.8%	49.7%	51.6%	51.6%

Long Term Google Buy Write Example

Like the previous Apple trade example, the Google Buy Write Analysis below reveals that selling a LEAPS call option provides substantial profits and downside protection. Selling the GOOG 600-Strike call option would result in $4,140 being credited to your brokerage account. This reduces your cost basis for purchasing 100 shares of Google stock. If GOOG stock closes at or above 600.0 at option expiration in January a $23,400 profit would be realized (before commission) which translates to a 63.9% return. This trade also provides good downside protection in the event Google stock declines in price. A 10% decline in the price of Google stock at option expiration to 366.66 would result in a positive .2% return.

GOOG					407.40 +3.18		
Dec 08, 2005 @ 15:14 ET (Data 15 Minutes Delayed)	*Bid 407.28 Ask 407.42 Size 1x1 Vol 6797308*						
Calls	**Bid**	**Ask**	**Open Int**	**Puts**	**Bid**	**Ask**	**Open Int**
08 Jan 570.0 (YVD AN)	47.70	48.40	535	08 Jan 570.0 (YVD MN)	174.90	175.90	115
08 Jan 580.0 (YVD AP)	45.50	46.20	952	08 Jan 580.0 (YVD MP)	183.00	184.00	196
08 Jan 590.0 (YVD AR)	43.40	44.20	204	08 Jan 590.0 (YVD MR)	191.20	192.10	104
08 Jan 600.0 (YVD AT)	41.40	42.20	1650	08 Jan 600.0 (YVD MT)	199.60	200.70	286

Buy Write Analysis

Buy Write Analysis

Stock Name	Current Stock Price	Call Strike	Call Price	Break Even
Google	407.4	600	41.4	366.00

New Analysis | Calculate | Print | Exit

% Change in Stock	-15.0%	-10.0%	-5.0%	0.0%	20.0%	40.0%	60.0%
Stock Price	346.29	366.66	387.03	407.40	488.88	570.36	651.84
Profit/Loss Stock	-6,111	-4,074	-2,037	0	8,148	16,296	24,444
Call Value	0.00	0.00	0.00	0.00	0.00	0.00	51.84
Profit/Loss Call	4,140	4,140	4,140	4,140	4,140	4,140	-1,044
Net Profit/Loss	-1,971	66	2,103	4,140	12,288	20,436	23,400
% Return	-5.4%	0.2%	5.7%	11.3%	33.6%	55.8%	63.9%

'Out-of-the-Money' Buy Write Versus an 'In-the-Money' Buy Write

There are many variations of buy write trading that depend on the strike price of the call option that is sold to establish the trade. In general, an 'in-the-money' buy write trade option provides more downside protection but less profit potential compared to an 'at-the-money' or 'out-of-the-money' buy write. An 'in-the-money' buy write trade can provide a profit even if there is a substantial price decline in the underlying stock. This is possible as the premium received from the sale of the call option compensates for the loss in value of the underlying stock.

An 'out-of-the-money' buy write provides more profit potential but less downside protection. As noted previously, writing an 'out-of-the-money' buy write call can provide a 50 to 60% return depending on the strike price of the call option sold.

Comparing Strike Prices

Let's examine the profit potential, percent return and downside protection for buy write trades over a range of call option strike prices. This will allow us to compare the profit potential of 'in-the-money' buy writes versus 'out-of-the-money' buy writes.

We will conduct this comparison using actual call option prices for Apple (AAPL) stock listed in the table below. Apple stock is currently trading at 74.08.

AAPL					74.08 +0.13				
Dec 08, 2005 (Data 15 Minutes Delayed)									
Calls	**Bid**	**Ask**	**Vol**	**Open Int**	**Puts**	**Bid**	**Ask**	**Vol**	**Open Int**
06 Apr 50.00 (QAA DJ	25.40	25.70	17	2804	06 Apr 50.00 (QAA PJ)	0.55	0.70	39	14597
06 Apr 60.00 (QAA DL	17.10	17.40	0	10631	06 Apr 60.00 (QAA PL)	2.10	2.25	3	6027
06 Apr 70.00 (QAA DN	10.60	10.80	63	5539	06 Apr 70.00 (QAA PN)	5.40	5.60	31	2001
06 Apr 80.00 (QAA DP	6.10	6.30	41	5462	06 Apr 80.00 (QAA PP)	10.80	11.10	30	386
06 Apr 90.00 (QAA DR	3.40	3.50	2	3718	06 Apr 90.00 (QAA PR)	18.10	18.30	55	216
06 Apr 100.0 (QAA DT	1.90	2.00	0	918	06 Apr 100.0 (QAA PT)	26.70	26.90	0	200

The table that follows compares the potential profit, percent return and downside protection over a range of Apple call option strikes from the April 60-Strike call to the April 90-Strike call. These sample trades are about 4½ months in duration.

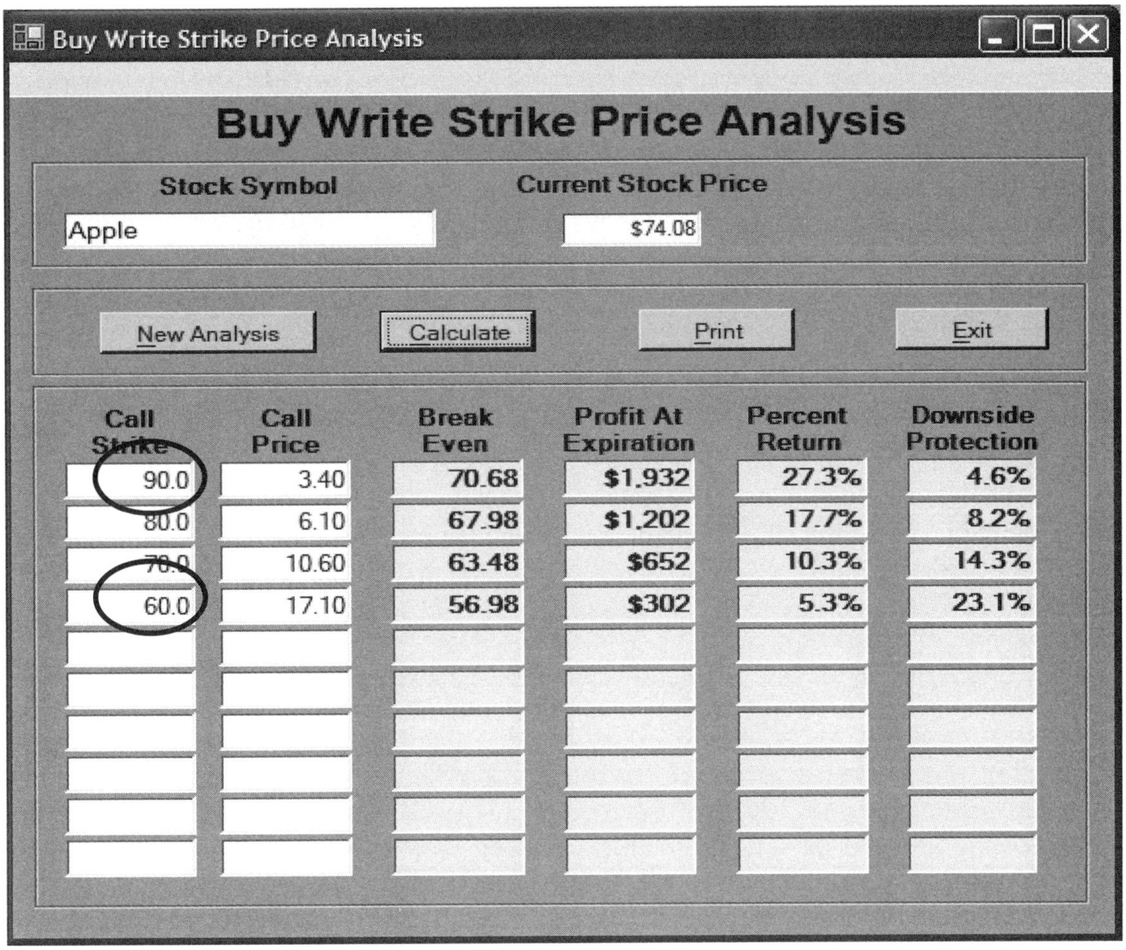

Buy Write Strike Price Analysis

<u>Top Row 90-Strike 'Out-of-the-Money' (Circled)</u>

Breakeven: 70.68 --- The breakeven price for the 90-Strike buy write is 70.68 and is calculated by subtracting the 3.40 call price from the 74.08 price of Apple stock. If Apple stock closes above 70.68 at option expiration a profit would be realized. If Apple stock closes below 70.68 a loss would incur.
Profit at Expiration: $1,932 --- A $1,932 profit will be realized on this trade if Apple stock closes at or above 90.0 at option expiration
Percent Return: 27.3% --- This trade will realize a 27.3% return with a $1,932 profit. This is calculated by dividing the $1,932 profit by the $7,068 cost of the buy write. The $7,068 cost is calculated subtracting the $340 received for selling the call option from the cost of purchasing 100 shares of Apple stock at 74.08.
Downside Protection: 4.6% --- This is the downside protection provided by the sale of the 90-Strike call option. Apple stock can decline 4.6% from its current price of 74.08 before the breakeven price of 70.68 is reached

Bottom Row 60-Strike 'In-the-Money' (Circled)

Breakeven: 56.98 --- The breakeven price for the 60-Strike buy write is 56.98 and is calculated by subtracting the 17.10 call price from the 74.08 price of Apple stock. If Apple stock closes above 56.98 at option expiration a profit would be realized. If Apple stock closes below 56.98 a loss would incur.
Profit at Expiration: $302 --- A $302 profit will be realized on this trade if Apple stock closes at or above 60.0 at option expiration
Percent Return: 5.3% --- This trade will realize a 5.3% return with a $302 profit. This is calculated by dividing the $302 profit by the $5,698 cost of the buy write. The $5,698 cost is calculated subtracting the $1,710 received for selling the call option from the cost of purchasing 100 shares of Apple stock at 74.08.
Downside Protect: 23.1% --- This is the downside protection provided by the sale of the 60-Strike call option. Apple stock can decline 23.1% from its current price of 74.08 before the breakeven price of 56.98 is reached

The preceding comparison table reveals that selling the 90-Strike 'out-of-the-money' call provides a much greater profit potential of $1,932 compared to the 'in-the-money' 60-Strike call which has a $302 profit potential. The 90-Strike call, however, provides less downside protection of 4.6% compared to the 60-Strike call which provides 23.1% protection. The 'at-the-money' 70-Strike call provides a 10.3% profit potential with 14.3% downside protection.

Note: The Strike Price Analysis tables presented in this Chapter are not required to implement the Buy Write Strategy. The tables are presented here to help compare the returns of 'out-of-the-money' versus 'in-the-money' buy write trades.

Strike Price Comparison for LEAPS Options

Let's examine a strike price comparison for long-term buy write trades using LEAPS options. The strike price comparison table below lists the profit potential, percent return and downside protection for the January Google LEAPS options listed in the option quote table below. The strike price comparison covered a range of call options from 'out-of-the-money' to 'in-the-money'. These options expire in about 25 months.

GOOG 407.40 +3.18

Dec 08, 2005 @ 15:14 ET (Data 15 Minutes Delayed)

Calls	Bid	Ask	Open	Puts	Bid	Ask	Open Int
08 Jan 260.0 (YWM AL-E)	186.60	187.50	182	08 Jan 260.0 (YWM ML-E)	15.40	16.00	73
08 Jan 300.0 (YVC AT-E)	159.30	160.40	362	08 Jan 300.0 (YVC MT-E)	25.10	25.60	388
08 Jan 340.0 (YVC AH-E)	134.90	135.90	185	08 Jan 340.0 (YVC MH-E)	37.90	38.40	569
08 Jan 440.0 (YVC AA-E)	87.20	87.90	120	08 Jan 440.0 (YVC MA-E)	84.50	85.20	46
08 Jan 480.0 (YVC AI-E)	72.60	73.40	210	08 Jan 480.0 (YVC MI-E)	109.00	109.70	105
08 Jan 520.0 (YVD AD-E)	60.30	61.10	52	08 Jan 520.0 (YVD MD-E)	136.50	137.30	64
08 Jan 560.0 (YVD AL-E)	50.00	50.90	175	08 Jan 560.0 (YVD ML-E)	167.00	167.80	33
08 Jan 600.0 (YVD AT-E)	41.40	42.20	1650	08 Jan 600.0 (YVD MT-E)	199.60	200.70	286

Buy Write Strike Price Analysis

Buy Write Strike Price Analysis

Stock Symbol: Google

Current Stock Price: $407.40

New Analysis | Calculate | Print | Exit

Call Strike	Call Price	Break Even	Profit At Expiration	Percent Return	Downside Protection
600.0	41.40	366.00	$23,400	63.9%	10.2%
560.0	50.00	357.40	$20,260	56.7%	12.3%
520.0	60.30	347.10	$17,290	49.8%	14.8%
480.0	72.60	334.80	$14,520	43.4%	17.8%
440.0	87.20	320.20	$11,980	37.4%	21.4%
340.0	134.90	272.50	$6,750	24.8%	33.1%
300.0	159.30	248.10	$5,190	20.9%	39.1%
260.0	186.60	220.80	$3,920	17.8%	45.8%

The Google long-term strike price comparison table covers a range of strike prices from 260 to 600. As expected this analysis reveals that selling LEAPS call options to enter buy write trades can provide substantial profits and significant downside protection. Selling the 'out-of-the-money' 600-Strike call option would provide your account with a $23,400 profit if Google stock closes at or above 600 at option expiration. This translates to a 63.9% return. This trade also provides good downside protection in the event Google stock declines in price.

Selling an 'in-the-money' 260-Strike call option would provide your account with a $18,660 cash credit which significantly reduces your cost of purchasing 100 shares of Google stock. Selling the 260-Strike call provides a hefty 45.8% downside protection. Google stock would have to decline more than 186.60 points to 220.80 at option expiration before a loss would be realized. This low risk buy write would provide a 17.8% return as long as Google stock closed at 260 or above at option expiration.

Each buy write investor must decide which strike price to sell when initiating a buy write trade to fit their individual risk tolerance. The trade examples just presented demonstrate that if you want a lower risk trade with increased downside protection then sell an 'in-the-money' call option. If you want a higher potential return with less downside protection then sell an 'out-of-the-money' call option.

In summary, there are three possible outcomes from buy write trading:

1. At option expiration, if the underlying stock closes at or above the strike price of the call sold, the stock will be 'called' and the buy write trade will realize its full profit potential.
2. At option expiration, if the underlying stock closes below the strike price of the call sold, the call will expire worthless and the investor maintains the stock in their brokerage account. At this point another buy write trade can be established by selling another call option.
3. If you want to keep your stock, the short call option can be closed out anytime before option expiration by buying back the call option 'to close'. You can then sell another call option to generate additional income.

Buy Write Summary

The buy write strategy offers you attractive income returns while providing some downside protection in the event the underlying stock declines in price. Stock selection and the timing of your entry are the most important factors for successful short-term buy write trading. These factors are less important with long-term buy write trading. Long-term buy writes reduce the risk of having to be 'right' about the short-term price direction of a stock, which is required when initiating short-term buy writes. The timing of 'when to enter' a LEAPS buy write trade is not as critical as the entry of a buy write trade with a short-term option expiration. LEAPS buy write trades have a one to three year period for favorable stock price movement before option expiration and also provide substantial down side protection if the underlying stock declines in price.

The preceding trade examples demonstrate that long-term buy write trading can realistically provide a 50 to 60% return or 30 to 40% downside protection depending on the strike price of the call option sold.

As with any stock option investment strategy, it is important to be diversified among different industries and not to concentrate all of your investment funds in just a few trades. Try to divide your investment funds among four to six stocks in different industries, so that a large loss in any one trade should not deplete your investment portfolio.

Chapter 8

Income Strategy

We learned in Chapter 7 that the *Buy Write Strategy* produces income by selling call option premium. Selling a call option results in cash being credited to your brokerage account. The sale of the call option also provides protection in the event the underlying stock declines in price. The buy write return analysis tables presented in the previous Chapter for Google and Apple revealed that selling an 'in-the-money' call option provides more downside protection but less profit than selling an 'out-of-the-money' call option. The goal of the *Income Strategy* is to purchase stock and sell an 'in-the-money' call option that provides good downside protection and a reasonable return. My trading experience shows that an annual return of 20 to 30% is realistic for this type of strategy.

Let's examine the first of four 'in-the-money' buy write income trades I took recently. On September 21st I purchased 100 shares of Akamai stock (AKAM) at 47.30 and sold one AKAM November 45-Strike call option at 5.70 (see copies of brokerage confirmations that follow). This option expires in about 2 months. The return analysis table for this income trade is included below.

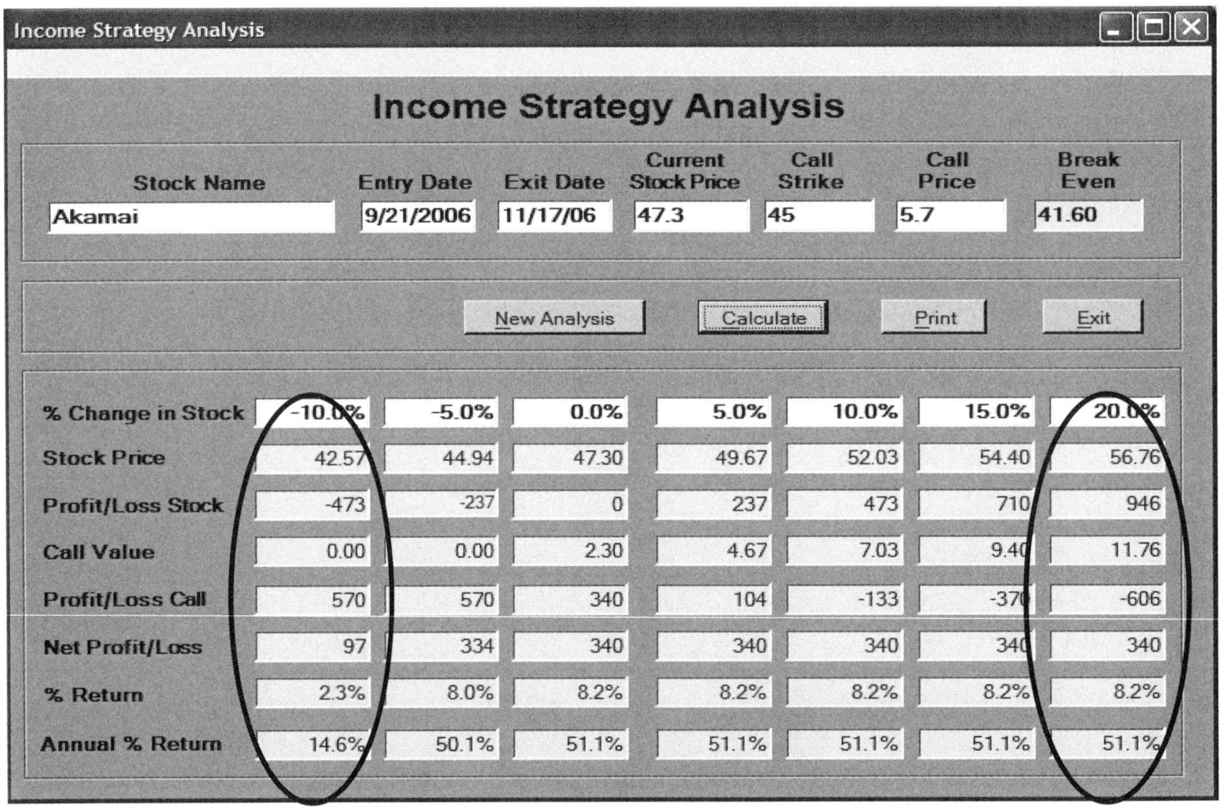

Income Strategy Analysis

Stock Name	Entry Date	Exit Date	Current Stock Price	Call Strike	Call Price	Break Even
Akamai	9/21/2006	11/17/06	47.3	45	5.7	41.60

New Analysis | Calculate | Print | Exit

% Change in Stock	-10.0%	-5.0%	0.0%	5.0%	10.0%	15.0%	20.0%
Stock Price	42.57	44.94	47.30	49.67	52.03	54.40	56.76
Profit/Loss Stock	-473	-237	0	237	473	710	946
Call Value	0.00	0.00	2.30	4.67	7.03	9.40	11.76
Profit/Loss Call	570	570	340	104	-133	-370	-606
Net Profit/Loss	97	334	340	340	340	340	340
% Return	2.3%	8.0%	8.2%	8.2%	8.2%	8.2%	8.2%
Annual % Return	14.6%	50.1%	51.1%	51.1%	51.1%	51.1%	51.1%

The preceding income trade analysis table displays the profit/loss potential over a range of prices for Akamai stock at option expiration from a 10% decline in the stock price to a 20% increase. The boxes below contain the analysis for Akamai income trade I took recently.

Akamai Income Trade Analysis

Left Hand Column – Stock Price Decline (Circled)

Stock % Change: -10% --- This assumes a 10% decline in the price of AKAM stock at option expiration
Stock Price: 42.57 --- The AKAM stock price after a 10% decline
Profit/Loss Stock: -473 --- The 100 shares of AKAM stock would realize a $473 loss if AKAM closes at 42.57 at option expiration
Call Value: 0 --- The AKAM 45-Strike call option would expire worthless if AKAM stock closes at 42.57 at option expiration
Profit/Loss Call: 570 --- The short 45-Strike call option produces a $570 profit if it expires worthless (sell call at 5.70 minus current value of 0 = +$570 profit)
Net Profit/Loss: 97 --- Combining the stock loss of $473 with the $570 profit from the call option results in an overall net profit of $97
Spread % Return: 2.3% --- The $97 profit represents a 2.3% return on the $4,160 investment required to establish this trade
Annual % Return: 14.6% --- The 2.3% return over the two month period translates to a 14.6% annualized return

Right Hand Column – Stock Price Increase (Circled)

Stock % Change: 20% --- This assumes a 20% increase in the price of AKAM stock at option expiration
Stock Price: 56.76 --- AKAM stock price after a 20% increase
Profit/Loss Stock: 946 --- The 100 shares of AKAM stock would realize a $946 profit if AKAM closes at 56.76 at option expiration
Call Value: 11.76 --- The AKAM 45-Strike call option would have an 11.76 value if AKAM stock closes at 56.76 at option expiration
Profit/Loss Call: -606 --- The short 45-Strike call option produces a $606 loss with a 11.76 value (sell at 5.70 minus current value of 11.76 = 6.06 loss)
Net Profit/Loss: 340 --- Combining the stock profit of $946 with the $606 loss from the call option results in an overall net profit of $340 for this trade
Spread % Return: 8.2% --- The $340 profit represents an 8.2% return on the $4,160 investment required to establish this trade
Annual % Return: 51.1% --- The 8.2% return over the two month period translates to a 51.1% annualized return

We can see from this analysis that this income trade provides limited profits and limited downside protection in the event Akamai stock declines in price. If Akamai stock closes at or above the 45-Strike price at option expiration, then the full profit potential of $340 will be realized and the 100 shares of Akamai stock will be 'called'. If AKAM stock closes substantially higher than 45 at option expiration then the profit would still be limited to $340 which equates to an 8.2% return over the two month period of this trade. If you were able to profitably 'rollover' this trade several times over the course of a year, the 8.2% return would translate to a 51% annualized yield. I normally buy to close the short call option prior to option expiration which allows me to keep my stock and sell another call option.

One real advantage of this trade is the increased downside protection provided by the sale of the 'in-the-money' call option. Selling the 'in-the-money' call option reduces the cost basis of AKAM stock from 47.30 to 41.60 allowing you to buy the stock at a discount. A 10% decline in AKAM stock at option expiration would still allow you to profit from this trade. The *Income Strategy* can offer attractive returns and ample downside protection resulting in a good balance between risk and reward.

Listed below is a profit potential summary for four income trades I took last week. These trades expire in about two months. Brokerage confirmations for these trades follow. The average annualized profit potential for these four trades is 34.5% demonstrating that the income strategy can offer both attractive returns and solid downside protection in the event of a modest price decline in the underlying stock.

Income Strategy Return Potential

Stock	Return Potential	Annualized Return
Mastercard	5.2%	32.4%
Akamai	8.2%	51.1%
Hewlett Packard	4.3%	27.0%
American Eagle	4.4%	27.7%
Average	5.5%	34.5%

Advantages of 'In-the-Money' Buy Writes versus 'Out-of-the-Money' Buy Writes

- Receive larger call option premiums that reduce cost basis of stock
- Lowers required investment costs and allows you to purchase stock at a discount
- Does not require large stock price increase to breakeven or profit
- Lower cost and increased downside protection results in a higher percentage of winning trades and reduces the severity of losing trades
- Can profit even if underlying stock declines in price
- Less overall risk
- Still receive dividends while holding stock

Disadvantages of 'In-the-Money' Buy Writes versus 'Out-of-the-Money' Buy Writes

- Lower annual percent profit return

E*TRADE FINANCIAL
Trading • Investing • Banking • Lending

E*TRADE Securities
Investment Account

TRADE CONFIRMATION

Account Name:

Account Type:

E*TRADE Securities LLC
P.O. Box 1542
Merrifield, VA 22116-1542
1-800-ETRADE-1 (1-800-387-2331)
etrade.com

Customer Update
Make sure your account information is up to date. Review/edit personal info at www.etrade.com (under the Accounts tab, click My Info) or by calling 1-800-ETRADE-1.

TRADE DATE	SETL DATE	MKT/CPT	SYMBOL/CUSIP	BUY/SELL	QUANTITY	PRICE	ACCT TYPE		
09/21/06	09/26/06	1 3	AKAM	BUY	100	$47.30	Margin	PRINCIPAL	$4,730.00
AKAMAI TECHNOLOGIES INC								COMMISSION	$7.99
								NET AMOUNT	$4,737.99
09/21/06	09/22/06	6 1	UMUK45	SELL	1	$5.70	Margin	PRINCIPAL	$570.00
CALL AKAMAI TECH NOV 045 ****								COMMISSION	$8.74
11/18/2006 EXPIRATION DATE								FEE	$0.02
OPEN CONTRACT								NET AMOUNT	$561.24

TRADE DATE	SETL DATE	MKT/CPT	SYMBOL/CUSIP	BUY/SELL	QUANTITY	PRICE	ACCT TYPE		
09/19/06	09/22/06	6 1	AEOS	BUY	100	$43.30	Margin	PRINCIPAL	$4,330.00
AMERICAN EAGLE OUTFITTERS INC NEW								COMMISSION	$7.99
								NET AMOUNT	$4,337.99
09/19/06	09/22/06	3 1	HPQ	BUY	100	$36.30	Margin	PRINCIPAL	$3,630.00
HEWLETT PACKARD CO								COMMISSION	$7.99
								NET AMOUNT	$3,637.99
09/19/06	09/20/06	5 1	AQUKH	SELL	1	$5.00	Margin	PRINCIPAL	$500.00
CALL AMERN EAGLE NOV 040 ****								COMMISSION	$8.74
11/18/2006 EXPIRATION DATE								FEE	$0.02
OPEN CONTRACT								NET AMOUNT	$491.24
09/19/06	09/20/06	5 1	HPQK35	SELL	1	$2.75	Margin	PRINCIPAL	$275.00
CALL HEWLETT PACK NOV 035 ****								COMMISSION	$8.74
11/18/2006 EXPIRATION DATE								FEE	$0.01
OPEN CONTRACT								NET AMOUNT	$266.25

TRADE DATE	SETL DATE	MKT/CPT	SYMBOL/CUSIP	BUY/SELL	QUANTITY	PRICE	ACCT TYPE		
09/20/06	09/25/06	6 1	MA	BUY	100	$66.55	Margin	PRINCIPAL	$6,655.00
MASTERCARD INC								COMMISSION	$7.99
								NET AMOUNT	$6,662.99
09/20/06	09/21/06	5 1	MAK65	SELL	1	$4.80	Margin	PRINCIPAL	$480.00
CALL MASTERCARD NOV 065 ****								COMMISSION	$8.74
11/18/2006 EXPIRATION DATE								FEE	$0.02
OPEN CONTRACT								NET AMOUNT	$471.24

Chapter 9

Profiting in Any Type of Market

Let's now examine option debit spreads which can profit in any type of market. Option debit spreads are implemented using only options by purchasing a call option and selling a call option with a higher strike price. Because the short option is 'covered' with the option purchase this would be a limited risk trade. Option debit spreads require considerably less trading capital than buy write trades as option spreads don't require the purchase of 100 shares of stock to implement the spread. We learned in Chapter 7 that buy write trades require the purchase of 100 shares of stock.

Profiting in Non-Trending Markets

Non-trending markets are difficult to trade and frustrate both bulls and bears. But traders who are able to adapt their strategies to non-trending markets can reap substantial profits from market price swings. When market volatility starts to increase, we shift our focus from option purchases to option spread trades.

The daily price chart below for Cleveland Cliffs (CLF) stock is an example of a non-trending market (price charts courtesy of Yahoo Finance). The percent gains and losses for Cleveland Cliffs stock over the past 7 weeks are listed below:

28.9% ***gain*** followed by a
33.8% ***loss*** followed by a
41.3% ***gain*** followed by a
24.0% ***loss*** followed by a
33.3% ***gain***

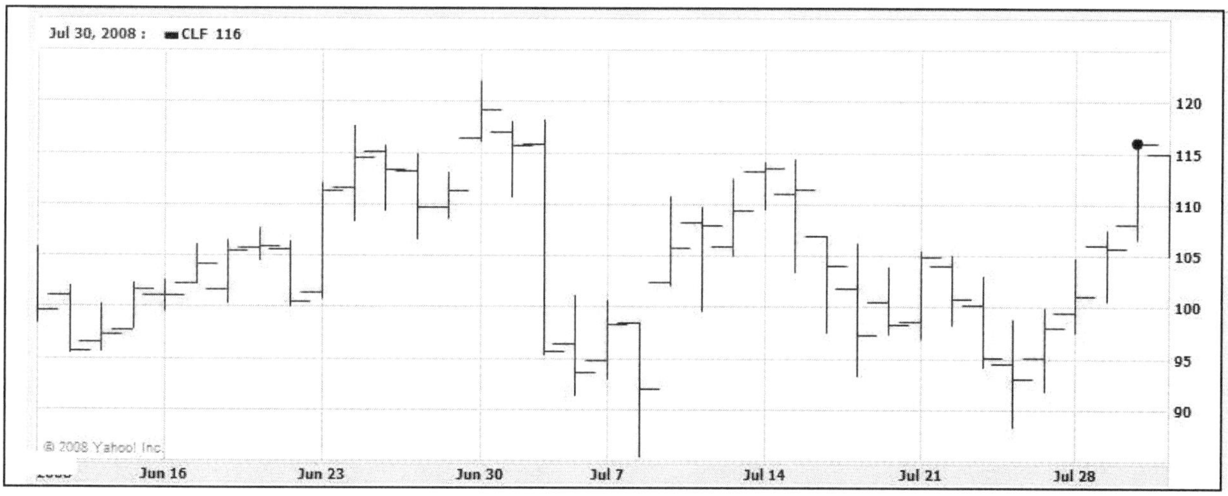

The net result of these volatile moves was that the price CLF stock was virtually unchanged over the 7 week period. A call or put option purchase strategy would have produced large losses over this period. The value of a put option would have decreased almost to zero during the 28.9%, 41.3% and 33.3% gains in CLF stock. And the value of a call option would have decreased almost to zero during the 33.8% and 24.0% losses in CLF stock. Over any two or three day period, the price of the stocks in your portfolio can increase or decrease 5% to 10%. If you have a leveraged option position and you are on the wrong side of one of these 10% price swings you can incur a large loss quickly.

We recommended a Cleveland Cliffs option spread trade in April to the members of our advisory service. Over this same 7 week period, the percent return for this recommended option spread trade never dropped below a +500% return. How was this return possible after such wide price swings?

Option Spreads versus Option Purchases

The call option purchase strategy presented in Chapter 6 can produce substantial profits if done correctly. We learned in Chapter 6 that when you purchase an out-of-the-money call option, the premium consists of only time value and the price of the underlying stock has to rise considerably (depending on the strike price of the call) in order to break-even on the trade. This is a result of the time decay characteristics of options as they approach expiration. Options lose all time value at option expiration. For example, today is August 20th and Apple stock is currently trading at 123.22. The Apple September 140-Strike call option is trading at 2.35 points and expires in about 5 weeks.

Buy Apple 140-Strike call option at 2.35 points

140.00 Strike
+ 2.35 Premium
= 142.35 Breakeven

Apple stock has to trade up to 142.35 at option expiration which is a 13.6% price increase before you break-even on this trade. If Apple does not close above 142.35 at option expiration then a total loss of the option premium will be realized making this purchase of an out-of-the-money call option a high risk investment. In-the-money call options have less time value than out-of-the-money calls. Purchasing an in-the-money option requires a much lower price increase in the underlying stock to break-even compared to an out-of-the-money call. Therefore the in-the-money call has a greater chance of being profitable and carries less risk.

There is a way to dramatically improve the risk/reward profile for option investing beyond purchasing in-the-money options. Option spreads completely change the risk/reward profile of option investing. Instead of purchasing an Apple call option today, let's look at establishing an option spread using Apple call options.

Today is August 20th and the Apple January 110-Strike call option is currently trading at 22.10 points and the January 120-Strike call is trading at 16.90. A call option spread can be created by buying the 110-Strike call and selling the 120-Strike call.

When you create an option spread by purchasing a call option and selling a related call option with a higher strike price:

- The call option purchased profits if the price of the underlying stock increases
- The call option sold profits if the price of the underlying stock decreases
- Your risk is limited to the cost of the spread

The table below displays the profit/loss potential for buying the Apple January 110-Strike call option for 22.10 points and selling the Apple January 120-Strike call for 16.90 points. The table displays profit results for various price changes for Apple stock at option expiration from a 15% increase to a 5% decline. Apple stock is trading at 123.22. If Apple stock increases 2.5% at option expiration to 126.30 a 92.3% return will be realized (circled).

<u>Apple Call Option Spread Analysis</u>
Buy 110-Strike Call Option @ 22.10
Sell 120-Strike Call Option @ <u>16.90</u>
Cost 5.20

Wealth Creation Alliance

Call Option Spread Analysis

Stock Symbol	Current Stock Price	Buy Strike	Buy Price	Sell Strike	Sell Price
AAPL	123.22	110	22.10	120	16.90

Cost: $5.20

Calculate | New Analysis | Print

% Change	15.0%	10.0%	5.0%	2.5%	0.0%	-2.5%	-5.0%
Stock Price	$141.70	$135.54	$129.38	$126.30	$123.22	$120.14	$117.06
Call Buy Value	$31.70	$25.54	$19.38	$16.30	$13.22	$10.14	$7.06
Call Sell Value	$-21.70	$-15.54	$-9.38	$-6.30	$-3.22	$-0.14	$0.00
Spread Value	$10.00	$10.00	$10.00	$10.00	$10.00	$10.00	$7.06
Spread Cost	$5.20	$5.20	$5.20	$5.20	$5.20	$5.20	$5.20
Spread Profit	$4.80	$4.80	$4.80	$4.80	$4.80	$4.80	$1.86
Spread % Ret	92.3%	92.3%	92.3%	92.3%	92.3%	92.3%	35.7%

The cost of this spread is $520 and is calculated by subtracting the 16.90 points we received from the sale of the 120-strike call from the 22.10 cost of the 110-strike call we purchased. The most we could lose on this spread trade is the $520 cost of the spread.

Let's take a look at how a 2½ percent increase in Apple stock to 126.30 results in a 92% return for this spread trade. If Apple stock increases 2.5% to 126.30 at option expiration, the option we purchased would lose value but the option we sold would increase in value and our spread would have a 10 point value. A 10 point spread value would result in a 4.80 point profit or $480 from our $520 purchase price. With a $520 cost, a $480 profit represents a 92% return. So in this example the option we purchased would realize a loss but the sale of the 120-strike call option allows us to make an overall profit on the spread trade.

If Apple stock remains flat at 123.22 at option expiration then a 92% return will be realized (circled). Again this is possible due to the profit on the sale of the 120-Strike call option.

Apple Stock Flat = 92.3% Return For Spread

Wealth Creation Alliance

Call Option Spread Analysis

Stock Symbol	Current Stock Price	Buy Strike	Buy Price	Sell Strike	Sell Price
AAPL	123.22	110	22.10	120	16.90

Cost: $5.20

Calculate | New Analysis | Print

% Change	15.0%	10.0%	5.0%	2.5%	0.0%	-2.5%	-5.0%
Stock Price	$141.70	$135.54	$129.38	$126.30	$123.22	$120.14	$117.06
Call Buy Value	$31.70	$25.54	$19.38	$16.30	$13.22	$10.14	$7.06
Call Sell Value	$-21.70	$-15.54	$-9.38	$-6.30	$-3.22	$-0.14	$0.00
Spread Value	$10.00	$10.00	$10.00	$10.00	$10.00	$10.00	$7.06
Spread Cost	$5.20	$5.20	$5.20	$5.20	$5.20	$5.20	$5.20
Spread Profit	$4.80	$4.80	$4.80	$4.80	$4.80	$4.80	$1.86
Spread % Ret	92.3%	92.3%	92.3%	92.3%	92.3%	92.3%	35.7%

And if Apple stock declines 5% to 117.06 a 35% return will be realized (circled). Profiting on a call option trade when the underlying stock declines in price is only possible because of the sale of the 120-strike call. This spread trade can be closed out anytime prior to option expiration by selling to close the 110-strike call and buying to close the 120-strike call. I will normally close out and take profits on a spread if the spread reaches 90 to 95% of its profit potential.

Apple Stock Declines 5% = 35.7% Return For Spread

Wealth Creation Alliance

Call Option Spread Analysis

Stock Symbol	Current Stock Price	Buy Strike	Buy Price	Sell Strike	Sell Price
AAPL	123.22	110	22.10	120	16.90

Cost: $5.20

Calculate | New Analysis | Print

% Change	15.0%	10.0%	5.0%	2.5%	0.0%	-2.5%	-5.0%
Stock Price	$141.70	$135.54	$129.38	$126.30	$123.22	$120.14	$117.06
Call Buy Value	$31.70	$25.54	$19.38	$16.30	$13.22	$10.14	$7.06
Call Sell Value	$-21.70	$-15.54	$-9.38	$-6.30	$-3.22	$-0.14	$0.00
Spread Value	$10.00	$10.00	$10.00	$10.00	$10.00	$10.00	$7.06
Spread Cost	$5.20	$5.20	$5.20	$5.20	$5.20	$5.20	$5.20
Spread Profit	$4.80	$4.80	$4.80	$4.80	$4.80	$4.80	$1.86
Spread % Ret	92.3%	92.3%	92.3%	92.3%	92.3%	92.3%	35.7%

So in this option trade example we would realize a 92% return on a call option trade if the price of Apple stock is flat at option expiration and a 35% return if Apple stock declines 5%. Profiting on a call option trade when the price of the underlying stock is flat or down reduces risk and results in a higher percentage of winning trades. The option spread strategy gives us a tremendous profit advantage compared to a strategy of just purchasing call options.

The Option Spread Strategy Gives Us a

Tremendous Profit Advantage and Less Risk

Compared to an Option Purchase Only Strategy

Profiting During the Recent Down Market

July 10th Dow Down 148 Points . . . July 20th Dow Down 149 Points . . .

July 24th Dow Down 226 Points . . . July 26th Dow Down 312 Points . . .

July 27th Dow Down 208 Points . . . July 31st Dow Down 146 Points . . .

August 3rd Dow Down 281 Points . . . August 9th Dow Down 387 Points . . .

August 14th Dow Down 207 Points . . . August 28th Dow Down 280 Points . . .

The call option spread strategy is an excellent way to profit during down markets or non-trending markets. As of August 29th the S&P 500 Index which is a broad measure of the US stock market is up 3.0% year to date. Despite the non-trending market the option spread strategy has been performing well. Remember that the call option you sell to create a spread profits as the price of the underlying stock declines providing profits during market declines.

Profit Potential Increases and Risk Decreases

The preceding Apple call option spread analysis demonstrates that the sale of the Apple 120-Strike call option increases the profit potential of the 110-Strike call option purchase and reduces risk. Unlike call option purchase trades this spread trade does not require a large price increase in the underlying stock to be profitable. This spread trade can be profitable even if the underlying stock decreases in price. The cost of this spread was $520 (per contract) and the maximum risk was $520 regardless of the price movement of Apple stock.

Apple Stock Goes ***Up*** 2.5% = 92% Option Spread Return

Apple Stock Stays ***Flat*** = 92% Option Spread Return

Apple Stock Goes ***Down*** 5% = 35% Option Spread Return

Maximum Risk = $520 Per Contract

Increasing Return Potential

When you initiate a call option spread trade, the option purchase and option sale can be done simultaneously or you can 'leg in' to the spread by purchasing an option first and selling an option with a higher strike price at a later date. If you purchase an option and the option increases in value, the sale of an option at a later date will increase the profit potential of the existing option purchase and provide down side protection in the event the underlying stock decreases in price. Let's look at an actual trade example to illustrate the return potential of 'legging in' to a spread trade.

Google symbol GOOG was on a WTL 'buy' signal. You can see from my brokerage confirmations bellow that on October 4th we purchased 18 Google 'in-the-money' 570-Strike call options at an average price of 37.35. The price of Google stock increased after the call option purchase and two weeks later on October 18th we sold to open 18 Google 640-Strike call options at an average price of 28.65. This resulted in $2,865 cash per contract being credited to my brokerage account.

Buy to Open 18 GOOG 570 Calls at an Average Price of 37.35
Sell to Open 18 GOOG 640 Calls at an Average Price of 28.65

Daily Account Activity

Trade Date	Settlement Date	Activity	Quantity	Trade #	Currency	Price
			PURCHASES AND SALES			
+GOPKQ:		Google Inc Cl A Nov 2007 570.00 Call				
10/04/2007	10/05/2007	Buy to Open	3.0000	47958637	USD	31.000000
10/04/2007	10/05/2007	Buy to Open	3.0000	47958639	USD	31.000000
10/04/2007	10/05/2007	Buy to Open	1.0000	47958641	USD	30.800000
10/05/2007	10/09/2007	Buy to Open	7.0000	48019599	USD	40.500000
10/08/2007	10/09/2007	Buy to Open	4.0000	48073360	USD	43.000000
+GOOKH:		Google Inc Cl A Nov 2007 640.00 Call				
10/18/2007	10/19/2007	Sell to Open	-1.0000	48631362	USD	28.800000
10/18/2007	10/19/2007	Sell to Open	-1.0000	48631364	USD	28.800000
10/18/2007	10/19/2007	Sell to Open	-2.0000	48631366	USD	28.800000
10/18/2007	10/19/2007	Sell to Open	-1.0000	48631368	USD	28.800000
10/18/2007	10/19/2007	Sell to Open	-5.0000	48632035	USD	28.600000
10/18/2007	10/19/2007	Sell to Open	-5.0000	48632037	USD	28.600000
10/18/2007	10/19/2007	Sell to Open	-2.0000	48632039	USD	28.600000
10/18/2007	10/19/2007	Sell to Open	-1.0000	48632041	USD	28.600000

The short sale of the 640-Strike call option was 'covered' by the purchase of the 570-Strike call option thereby limiting my risk to the cost of the spread. The cost of the spread is calculated by subtracting the sale price from the buy price and in this example is 8.70 points or $870.

Buy Price of 37.35 Minus Sale Price of 28.65 = Maximum Risk of $870

At the time the 640-Strike call option was sold, Google stock was trading at 639. The 640-Strike call option was an 'out-of-the-money' option as the strike price was greater than the stock price.

Strike Price of 640 and Stock Price of 639 = 'Out-of-the-Money' Option

Out-of-the-money options consist of only time value and no intrinsic value. Shorting an out-of-the-money option that consists of only time value takes full advantage of the 'time decay' characteristics of options. In this example the out-of-the-money 640-Strike call that I sold for 28.65 points is all time value which will decay to zero and will result in a 28.65 point ($2,865) profit per contract at option expiration regardless of the price movement of Google stock.

Selling an Option at 28.65 and Later Buying Back at Zero = 28.65 Point Profit

Short 28.65 Points of Time Value = 28.65 Points of Profit at Option Expiration

The full profit potential for this spread will be realized if Google stock closes at or above the strike price of the option that was sold at option expiration. In this example if Google stock closes at or above 640 the full profit potential of 61.30 points ($6,130) per contract will be realized.

The profit potential is calculated by subtracting the 8.70 point cost of the spread from the difference between the strike price of the option sold (640) and the strike price of the option purchased (570).

640 Sell Strike – 570 Buy Strike – 8.70 Cost = 61.30 Profit Potential

The Call Option Spread Analysis that follows displays the profit/loss potential for buying the Google 570-Strike call for 37.35 points and selling the out-of-the-money Google 640-Strike call for 28.65 points. The table displays profit results for various price changes for Google stock at option expiration from a 10% increase to a 5% decline.

Google stock is trading at 639. If Google stock increases 2.5% at option expiration to 654.98 a 704.6% return will be realized (circled). If Google is trading at 654.98 at option expiration, the option purchase would increase in value to 84.98 and the option sold would incur a 14.98 point loss, resulting in a 70.0 point net spread value (84.98 – 14.98 = 70.0). A 70.0 point spread value would result in a 61.30 point profit with an 8.70 point cost. With an 8.70 cost, a 61.30 profit represents a 704% return.

Google Stock Increases 2.5% = 704% Option Return

Wealth Creation Alliance

Call Option Spread Analysis

Stock Symbol	Current Stock Price	Buy Strike	Buy Price	Sell Strike	Sell Price
GOOG	639.00	570	37.35	640	28.65

Cost: $8.70

Calculate | New Analysis | Print

% Change	15.0%	10.0%	5.0%	2.5%	0.0%	-2.5%	-5.0%
Stock Price	$734.85	$702.90	$670.95	$654.98	$639.00	$623.03	$607.05
Call Buy Value	$164.85	$132.90	$100.95	$84.98	$69.00	$53.02	$37.05
Call Sell Value	$-94.85	$-62.90	$-30.95	$-14.98	$0.00	$0.00	$0.00
Spread Value	$70.00	$70.00	$70.00	$70.00	$69.00	$53.02	$37.05
Spread Cost	$8.70	$8.70	$8.70	$8.70	$8.70	$8.70	$8.70
Spread Profit	$61.30	$61.30	$61.30	$61.30	$60.30	$44.32	$28.35
Spread % Ret	704.6%	704.6%	704.6%	704.6%	693.1%	509.5%	325.9%

And if Google stock remains flat at 639 at option expiration then a 693% return will be realized (circled below). A 5% decline in Google stock to 607.05 results in a 325% return (circled).

Wealth Creation Alliance

Call Option Spread Analysis

Stock Symbol	Current Stock Price	Buy Strike	Buy Price	Sell Strike	Sell Price
GOOG	639.00	570	37.35	640	28.65

Cost: $8.70

Calculate | New Analysis | Print

% Change	15.0%	10.0%	5.0%	2.5%	0.0%	-2.5%	-5.0%
Stock Price	$734.85	$702.90	$670.95	$654.98	$639.00	$623.03	$607.05
Call Buy Value	$164.85	$132.90	$100.95	$84.98	$69.00	$53.02	$37.05
Call Sell Value	$-94.85	$-62.90	$-30.95	$-14.98	$0.00	$0.00	$0.00
Spread Value	$70.00	$70.00	$70.00	$70.00	$69.00	$53.02	$37.05
Spread Cost	$8.70	$8.70	$8.70	$8.70	$8.70	$8.70	$8.70
Spread Profit	$61.30	$61.30	$61.30	$61.30	$60.30	$44.32	$28.35
Spread % Ret	704.6%	704.6%	704.6%	704.6%	693.1%	509.5%	325.9%

85% Increase in Profit Potential

Profiting on a call option trade when the underlying stock declines in price is only possible because of the sale of the 640-strike call option. When the 640-Strike call option was sold the existing 570-Strike option purchase had a 33.70 point open trade profit. Selling the out-of-the-money 640-Strike call for 28.65 points resulted in an 85% increase in profit potential of the 570-Strike purchase.

The sale of the 640-Strike call also provides downside protection in the event Google stock declines in price. For example, if Google stock declined 8% at option expiration to 587.88 the value of the 570-Strike call would be 17.88 points and the 570-Strike call purchase would incur a 52% loss of the 37.35 purchase price. The spread trade, however, would realize a 105% profit.

This option trade can be closed out any time prior to option expiration by selling the 570-strike call to close and buying to close the 640-strike call. We will normally close out and take profits on a spread if the spread reaches 90 to 95% of its profit potential.

The Call Option Spread Analysis for the Google trade demonstrates the attractive profit potential for the *Call Option Spread Strategy*:

- Profit Potential of $110,340 ($6,130 Per Option X 18 Options)
- 704% Option Return if Google Stock is Up 2.5% at Option Expiration
- 693% Option Return if Google Stock is Flat at Option Expiration
- 325% Option Return if Google Stock is Down 5% at Option Expiration
- Maximum Risk of $870 Per Option

Call option spread trades have several advantages compared to call option purchase trades:

1) Increased Profit Potential
A limited risk call option spread is created by purchasing a call option and selling a call option with a higher strike price. The sale of a call option can increase the profit potential of an existing option purchase by 40% to 60% on average. In the Google spread trade example just presented, the sale of the 640-Strike call increased the profit potential of the 570-Strike call purchase by 85%.

2) The Call Option Sale Provides Downside Protection
The sale of a call option results in cash being credited to your brokerage account. This reduces the cost basis of the option purchase and provides downside protection in the event the price of the underlying stock declines in price.

Let's take another look at the recent price swings for CLF stock.

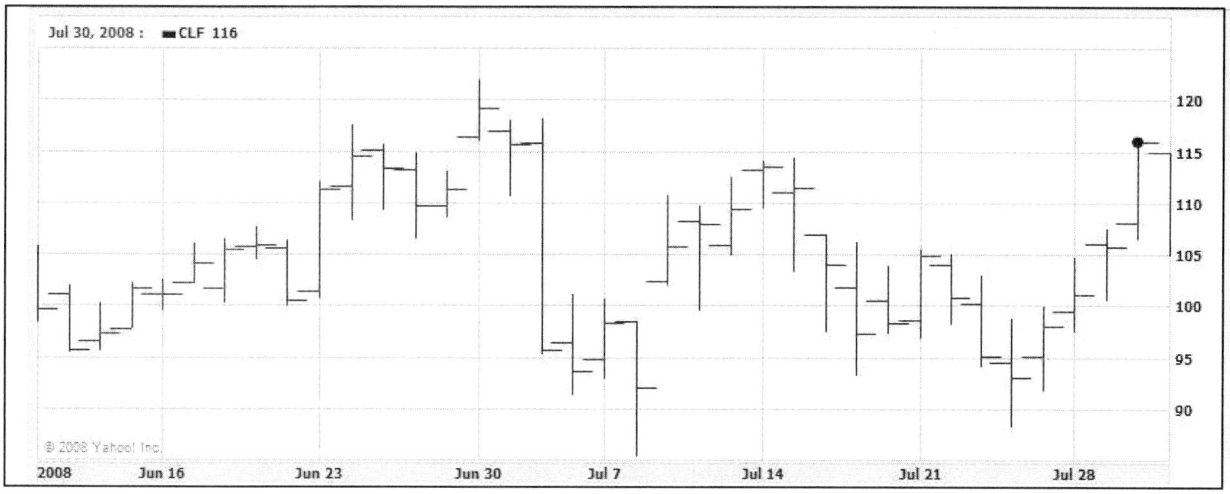

We recommended to the members of our advisory service the purchase of the CLF 50-Strike call option at 19.75 points on April 3rd and the sale of the CLF 65-Strike call at 19.45 points two weeks later on April 17th. The sale of the 65-Strike call profits if CLF stock declines in price. CLF stock would have to decline more than 36% at option expiration before a loss would be realized on this spread trade.

Wealth Creation Alliance

Call Option Spread Analysis

Stock Symbol	Current Stock Price	Buy Strike	Buy Price	Sell Strike	Sell Price
CLF	79.40	50	19.75	65	19.45

Cost $0.30

Calculate | New Analysis | Print

% Change	30.0%	20.0%	10.0%	0.0%	-10.0%	-20.0%	-30.0%
Stock Price	$103.22	$95.28	$87.34	$79.40	$71.46	$63.52	$55.58
Call Buy Value	$53.22	$45.28	$37.34	$29.40	$21.46	$13.52	$5.58
Call Sell Value	$-38.22	$-30.28	$-22.34	$-14.40	$-6.46	$0.00	$0.00
Spread Value	$15.00	$15.00	$15.00	$15.00	$15.00	$13.52	$5.58
Spread Cost	$0.30	$0.30	$0.30	$0.30	$0.30	$0.30	$0.30
Spread Profit	$14.70	$14.70	$14.70	$14.70	$14.70	$13.22	$5.28
Spread % Ret	4,900.0%	4,900.0%	4,900.0%	4,900.0%	4,900.0%	4,406.7%	1,760.0%

3) Reduces Risk Substantially

Purchasing the CLF 50-Strike call at 19.75 points incurs a risk of $1,975. If CLF stock closes below 50.0 at option expiration then the full $1,975 premium would be lost. But with the sale of the 65-Strike call at 19.45 points, our maximum risk for the spread is limited to the cost of the spread which in this example would be .30 points or $30 regardless of the price movement of CLF stock.

19.75 Cost of 50-Strike call purchase
-19.45 Sale of 65-Strike call
.30 Cost of spread

4) Allows You to Maintain Positions During Volatile Markets

We use money management stops with the option purchase strategy. We normally will exit an option trade if the value of the option drops 20% to 30% below our purchase price. This allows us to exit a losing option trade before it develops into a large loss which can devastate a portfolio and can force you out of the option investing game completely. Remember that if you incur a 50% loss, you must achieve a 100% gain just to break even.

Exiting losing trades before they develop into large losses is an essential requirement of any successful trading strategy. During the recent price swings in CLF stock a call option purchase strategy would have forced us to sell CLF call options during the 33.8% and 24% CLF stock price decreases in order to avoid large losses. But the CLF option spread trade maintained a profit during the recent price swings in CLF stock and we were not forced to sell the option spread.

5) Spreads Can Be Profitable If a Stock Goes Up or Down

Option spreads can be profitable if the underlying stock price increases, decreases or remains flat at option expiration. In the CLF spread example, the spread would be profitable if the price of CLF stock increases, remains flat or decreases 35% at option expiration. The CLF spread would not turn into a loss unless CLF stock decreases more than 36% at option expiration.

Average Return of 552.7% in Difficult Market

The option spread strategy has the best overall risk/reward profile during non-trending markets. We make option spread recommendations for the members of our advisory services. The profit/loss table below lists the open trade profit results as of July 30th for all of the recommended spread trades. The table lists the buy price, number of option contracts, current price, dollar profit and percent profit for each option spread recommendation. The composite portfolio of all spread trades currently has a $130,068 profit and an average return of 552.7% demonstrating the powerful profit potential of option spread trading. All of the recommended spread trades are profitable with no losing trades.

Open Trade Profit Results as of July 30th

Option Spread	Entry	Quantity	Last	Gain	Percent
Portfolio	Price		Price		Gain
Basic Matrls Co Jan 50 call	$25.10	4	$33.05	$3,180	31.7%
Basic Matrls Co Jan 80 call	$25.25	-4	$15.05	$4,080	40.4%
Oil Drilling Co Sep 30 call	$14.00	8	$30.95	$13,560	121.1%
Oil Drilling Co Sep 55 call	$12.60	-8	$10.45	$1,720	17.1%
Oil Service Co Sep 50 call	$11.50	9	$6.30	-$4,680	-45.2%
Oil Service Co Sep 60 call	$10.50	-9	$1.60	$8,010	84.8%
Steel Co Oct 50 call	$19.75	6	$65.85	$27,660	233.4%
Steel Co Oct 65 call	$19.45	-6	$51.65	-$19,320	-165.6%
Inds Metals Jan 45 call	$21.40	5	$46.65	$12,625	118.0%
Inds Metals Jan 70 call	$13.80	-5	$28.85	-$7,525	-109.1%
Oil Explor Jan 105 call	$25.50	4	$45.85	$8,140	79.8%
Oil Explor Jan 140 call	$24.90	-4	$22.30	$1,040	10.4%
Computer Co Jan 130 call	$44.40	3	$38.50	-$1,770	-13.3%
Computer Co Jan 160 call	$40.00	-3	$20.45	$5,865	48.9%
Genomics Co Jan 65 call	$21.50	5	$59.40	$18,950	176.3%
Genomics CoJan 90 call	$18.50	-5	$37.95	-$9,725	-105.1%
Oil Srvs Co Jan 60 call	$25.10	4	$26.45	$540	5.4%
Oil Srvs Co Jan 80 call	$19.10	-4	$13.85	$2,100	27.5%

Open Trade Profit Results as of July 30th Continued

Option Spread Portfolio	Entry Price	Quantity	Last Price	Gain	Percent Gain
Steel Co Sep 15 call	$6.20	16	$7.05	$1,360	13.7%
Steel Co Sep 22.5 call	$4.63	-16	$1.40	$5,168	69.8%
Oil Srvs Co Jan 25 call	$11.10	9	$13.75	$2,385	23.9%
Oil Srvs Co Jan 40 call	$8.75	-9	$3.70	$4,545	57.7%
Ag Co Jan 70 call	$42.30	3	$65.20	$6,870	54.1%
Ag Co Jan 100 call	$33.60	-3	$41.95	-$2,505	-24.9%
Fncl Servs Co Jan 140 call	$43.80	3	$134.00	$27,060	205.9%
Fncl Servs Co Jan 180 call	$40.00	-3	$99.00	-$17,700	-147.5%
Drug Store Co Jan 40 call	$9.50	6	$9.95	$270	4.7%
Drug Store Co Jan 50 call	$7.65	-6	$3.70	$2,370	51.6%
Comm Co Jan 80 call	$33.30	3	$43.42	$3,036	30.4%
Comm Co Jan 110 call	$32.60	-3	$22.77	$2,949	30.2%
Defense Co Sep 55 call	$11.00	4	$24.10	$5,240	119.1%
Defense Co Sep 65 call	$11.10	-4	$13.90	-$1,120	-25.2%
Basic Matrls Co Jan 40 call	$12.90	8	$18.50	$4,480	43.4%
Basic Matrls Co Jan 55 call	$13.80	-8	$10.15	$2,920	26.4%
Coal Co Jan 40 call	$18.60	6	$47.30	$17,220	154.3%
Coal Co Jan 50 call	$18.20	-6	$39.25	-$12,630	-115.7%
Oil Srvs Co Jan 35 call	$15.10	7	$23.00	$5,530	52.3%
Oil Srvs Co Jan 45 call	$13.60	-7	$15.20	-$1,120	-11.8%
Fertilizer Co Jan 30 call	$15.80	7	$23.35	$5,285	47.8%
Fertilizer Co Jan 55 call	$11.40	-7	$8.10	$2,310	28.9%
Credit Card Co Jan 155 Call	$37.40	3	$112.00	$22,380	199.5%
Credit Card Co Jan 185 call	$37.70	-3	$86.65	-$14,685	-129.8%
Total Profit / Average Gain				**$136,068.00**	**552.7%**

Option Strategy Profit Results

The table below lists the current open trade profit results for our advisory service option trade recommendations. The table lists the buy price, number of option contracts, current price, dollar profit and percent profit for each option recommendation. There are currently $397.958.00 in open trade profits and an average return of 497.6% for the option trade recommendations.

Advisory Service Option Strategy
Current Profits: $397,958.00 and 497.6% Return

Option	Entry Price	Qty	Last Price	Profit	Percent Profit
Department Stores Mar 55 call	$13.50	7	$14.30	$ 560	5.9%
Regional Banks Apr 35 call	$0.90	18	$10.12	$ 16,596	1024.4%
Nasdaq Apr 85 call	$12.87	6	$21.92	$ 5,430	70.3%
Health Care Plans Mar 80 call	$20.35	5	$22.68	$ 1,165	11.4%
Home Improvement Mar 85 call	$3.49	24	$26.88	$ 56,136	670.2%
Aerospace Mar 100 call	$3.72	5	$49.42	$ 22,850	1228.5%
Credit Services Apr 75 call	$1.74	124	$12.35	$ 131,564	609.8%
Electronic Equipment Apr 95 call	$5.25	4	$32.27	$ 10,808	514.7%
Grocery Stores Apr 45 call	$9.10	7	$27.85	$ 13,125	206.0%
Entertainment Mar 75 call	$14.67	5	$29.23	$ 7,280	99.3%
Credit Services 2 Mar 225 call	$1.23	10	$44.75	$ 43,520	3538.2%
Financial ETF Mar 115 call	$0.57	12	$33.33	$ 39,312	5747.4%
Telecom Services Feb 33 call	$0.40	8	$16.07	$ 12,536	3917.5%
Health Care Mar 54 call	$0.50	23	$16.62	$ 37,076	3224.0%
Total Profit / Avg Gain				$397,958.00	497.6%

If you would like to learn more about becoming a member of our advisory service then log on to www.WeeklyOptionAlert.com or call our sales partner Brad toll free at (866)-661-5664 or (310)-647-5664. Click the 'Trade Results' link for updated profit performance for the trading strategies.

Log On to www.WeeklyOptionAlert.com or

Call Brad toll free (866)-661-5664 or (310)-647-5664

Click Trade Results for Updated Profit Performance

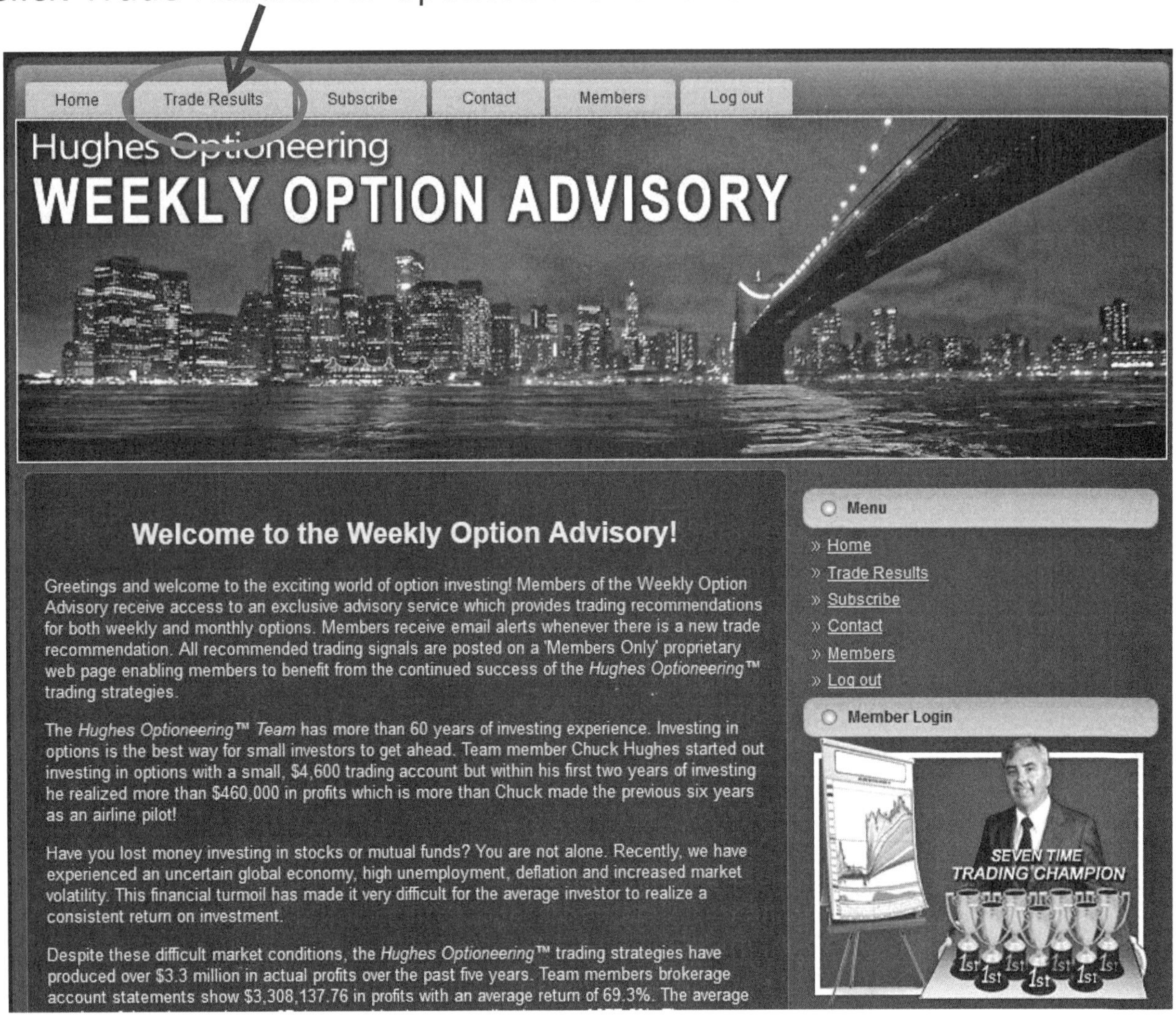

The Legacy Continues

Thank you for joining me on our journey. I hope that you were able to gather some new concepts for your investment portfolio. Investing in the markets can be a very complex, anxiety provoking and risky endeavor. I am hoping that I was able to simplify a lot of concepts for the novice trader and at the same time challenge the more seasoned trader with a different perspective. For the novice trader, it often helps to follow the market and to track different potential purchases before jumping in and going fully operational. There is a saying that goes "bet with your head and not your heart". I like to apply the same thought to investing. Always invest with your head. Remember patience is an ally in investing. Call on and use this virtue often.

Many thanks go out to Chuck Hughes and all his contributions to this book. I am grateful for his years of mentoring and his endless patience with this project. Hopefully, this is our first collaborative book of many.

My grandfather and father's investing legacy continues on after their deaths. What they were able to gain through prudent investing continues to provide our family with comfort and security. My goal is to continue this legacy of learning, teaching and growing so the following generations may continue with our family's dreams. This will be my legacy. Welcome to the Legacy Family and good luck on your journey!

Regards For Now,

John Weston

Thank you for giving me the opportunity to share with you some of my insights in the world of stock and option investing. It's been my pleasure to work with John over the years and watch him learn, embrace, and develop his own tools of our profession. Thanks for taking the time to share with me my love of investing. I hope you have found the investing world as fascinating as I do. Good luck with your Shoestring Millionaire portfolio and 'Here's to Prosperity!'

Sincerely,

Chuck Hughes

Appendix

$1,051,750.14 In Actual Profits

The account statements and tax schedules included here and on Page 57 reveal that the *Shoestring Millionaire Trading Strategies* helped me accumulate $1,051,750.14 in trading profits and income over the past 24 months. This has provided me with 'peace of mind' knowing that my family is financially secure. One half of my trading accounts are retirement accounts or educational trust accounts for my children.

BROWN|CO

ONE BEACON STREET, BOSTON, MA 02108-3102

Page: 1 of 20

Your Monthly Brokerage Account Statement — March 31, 2006 - April 28, 2006

Valuation Summary

Account Value: **$506,439.79**

	This Period	Year-to-date
Beginning Account Value	**$467,825.57**	**$399,543.98**
Income Received	109.02	502.82
Expenses Paid	-18.88	-158.66
Change in Account Value	38,440.20	106,063.19
Miscellaneous / Other	83.88	488.46
Ending Account Value	**$506,439.79**	**$506,439.79**

Realized Gain/Loss Summary

	This Period	Year-to-date
Total Short Term Gain/Loss	-24,897.68	48,954.29
Total Realized Gain/Loss	**-$24,897.68**	**$48,954.29**

Please refer to forms 1099 during tax season to provide tax reporting information. Realized Gain/Loss excludes transactions for which we have insufficient data.

Portfolio Summary

	Market Value on 03/31/06	Market Value on 04/28/06	Unrealized Gain/Loss	% of Portfolio
Cash/Margin	-6,026.43	5,986.79		1
Money Balance	**-$6,026.43**	**$5,986.79**		**1**
Long Equities	97,867.00	90,518.00	11,922.00	18
Long Options	405,555.00	419,590.00	116,597.00	81
Short Options	-29,570.00	-9,655.00	-4,335.13	
Equities and Options	**$473,852.00**	**$500,453.00**	**$124,183.87**	**99**
Total Account Value *	**$467,825.57**	**$506,439.79**	**$124,183.87**	**100**

E*TRADE FINANCIAL

QUOTES GO | SEARCH GO Help Center | Open an Account LOG OFF

Accounts | **Trading & Portfolios** | Quotes & Research | Mutual Funds, ETFs, & Bonds | Retirement & Advice | Banking & Credit Cards | Mortgages & Home Equity

Trade Portfolios View Orders | Balances | Transaction History | Account Records | Power E*TRADE

May 11, 2006 12:03 PM ET

Portfolios

Alerts | Transfer Money | Bill Pay | Help

Portfolios | Performance & Value | Positions | Gains & Losses | Risk Analyzer

Account/Watch List: LEGACY PUBLISHING LLC Create / Edit List **View:** Performance Customize

Market Value: $563,590.74 ($161,283.56 / 40.09%) **DJIA** 11,531.95 ▼ -110.70 **Nasdaq** 2,284.05 ▼ -36.69

REFRESH | STREAMING QUOTES | EXPORT TO EXCEL

Symbol		Current Price	Change $	Change %	Day's Gain	Qty	Price Paid	Total Gain $	Total Gain %	Market Val	Edit
⊞ BHPAH	Trade	**12.40**	1.00	8.77%	$1,200.00	12	$9.60	$[illegible],335.02	28.[illegible]9%	$14,880.00	Edit
⊞ BHPKH	Trade	**11.60**	0.60	5.45%	$360.00	6	$8.40	$1,907.51	37.75%	$6,960.00	Edit
⊞ CBGIK	Trade	**31.90**	0.00	0.00%	$0.00	8	$18.70	$10,538.02	70.34%	$25,520.00	Edit
CBGIL	Trade	**27.30**	0.00	0.00%	$0.00	4	$18.00	$3,709.01	51.44%	$10,920.00	Edit
CBGIM	Trade	**24.50**	0.00	0.00%	$0.00	4	$19.00	$2,189.01	28.76%	$9,800.00	Edit
CRSLB	Trade	**38.20**	0.00	0.00%	$0.00	2	$33.50	$930.51	13.87%	$7,640.00	Edit
⊞ EEMIR	Trade	**22.50**	0.00	0.00%	$0.00	6	$17.95	$2,709.52	25.11%	$13,500.00	Edit
EEMLR	Trade	**21.50**	-1.40	-6.11%	-$420.00	3	$20.20	$379.76	6.26%	$6,450.00	Edit
⊞ EWCIG	Trade	**4.80**	0.00	0.00%	$0.00	36	$4.40	$1,389.03	8.74%	$17,280.00	Edit
⊞ FTIJJ	Trade	**20.90**	0.00	0.00%	$0.00	13	$13.89	$9,076.28	50.16%	$27,170.00	Edit
⊞ IOKIZ	Trade	**30.50**	0.00	0.00%	$0.00	4	$29.80	$261.02	2.19%	$12,200.00	Edit
⊞ OIIJJ	Trade	**27.60**	0.00	0.00%	$0.00	6	$22.35	$3,129.52	23.30%	$16,560.00	Edit
⊞ OMUAE	Trade	**13.00**	0.28	2.20%	$336.00	12	$11.80	$1,415.02	9.98%	$15,600.00	Edit
⊞ OPQAN	Trade	**29.80**	0.00	0.00%	$0.00	6	$27.75	$1,205.52	7.23%	$17,880.00	Edit
OPQAQ	Trade	**26.10**	0.00	0.00%	$0.00	3	$28.50	-$730.24	-8.53%	$7,830.00	Edit
OYGAF	Trade	**49.00**	0.00	0.00%	$0.00	6	$13.30	$21,405.51	267.75%	$29,400.00	Edit
⊞ OYGAG	Trade	**41.00**	0.00	0.00%	$0.00	12	$19.97	$25,205.03	105.04%	$49,200.00	Edit
⊞ OYZAJ	Trade	**26.00**	0.10	0.39%	$90.00	9	$22.00	$3,569.28	18.00%	$23,400.00	Edit
RTILL	Trade	**25.60**	2.20	9.40%	-$10.24	3	$25.60	-$10.24	-0.13%	$7,680.00	Edit

Symbol		Current Price	Change $	Change %	Day's Gain	Qty	Price Paid	Total Gain $	Total Gain %	Market Val	Edit
⊞ RTPJB	Trade	**43.50**	0.00	0.00%	$0.00	2	$42.75	$132.52	1.55%	$8,700.00	Edit
⊞ TIEIG	Trade	**47.50**	0.00	0.00%	$0.00	10	$15.40	$32,076.52	207.97%	$47,500.00	Edit
⊞ TNBIH	Trade	**13.00**	0.00	0.00%	$0.00	15	$11.97	$1,514.78	8.42%	$19,500.00	Edit
⊞ VHFAL	Trade	**23.80**	0.00	0.00%	$0.00	6	$22.40	$819.52	6.09%	$14,280.00	Edit
VOHAI	Trade	**14.90**	-0.10	-0.67%	-$10.99	4	$14.90	-$10.99	-0.18%	$5,960.00	Edit
⊞ VOIAK	Trade	**35.70**	0.00	0.00%	$0.00	4	$22.60	$5,227.01	57.74%	$14,280.00	Edit
⊞ VOIAM	Trade	**26.10**	-0.60	-2.25%	-$480.00	8	$20.35	$4,578.02	28.08%	$20,880.00	Edit
⊞ ZAMAJ	Trade	**5.50**	-0.20	-3.51%	-$400.00	20	$5.30	$369.02	3.47%	$11,000.00	Edit
ZBKAE	Trade	**19.90**	-0.70	-3.40%	-$420.00	6	$11.30	$5,147.76	75.79%	$11,940.00	Edit
ZBKAX	Trade	**21.80**	0.10	0.46%	$240.00	24	$14.70	$17,021.01	48.22%	$52,320.00	Edit
⊞ ZSTAH	Trade	**11.90**	0.00	0.00%	$0.00	15	$10.60	$1,914.78	12.02%	$17,850.00	Edit
⊞ ZZTAK	Trade	**24.70**	3.10	14.35%	$919.76	6	$23.20	$879.52	6.31%	$14,820.00	Edit
Cash						4,690.74				$4,690.74	
				Totals	$1,404.53		$402,307.18	$161,283.56	40.09%	$563,590.74	

LEGEND: ⊞ **collapsed** (click to expand) ⊟ **expanded** (click to collapse)

Real-time quotes

E*TRADE FINANCIAL QUOTES GO | SEARCH GO Help Center | Open an Account LOG OFF

Accounts | Trading & Portfolios | Quotes & Research | Mutual Funds, ETFs, & Bonds | Retirement & Advice | Banking & Credit Cards | Mortgages & Home Equity

Trade Portfolios View Orders | Balances | Transaction History | Account Records | Power E*TRADE

May 09, 2006 8:47 PM ET

Portfolios

Alerts | Transfer Money | Bill Pay | Help

Portfolios | Performance & Value | Positions | Gains & Losses | Risk Analyzer

Account/Watch List: LEGACY PUBLISHING LLC Create / Edit List

View: Performance Customize

Market Value: $174,935.36 ($53,103.97 / 43.59%)

DJIA 11,639.77 ▲ +55.23 **Nasdaq** 2,338.25 ▼ -6.74

REFRESH | STREAMING QUOTES | EXPORT TO EXCEL

Symbol		Current Price	Change $	Change %	Day's Gain	Qty	Price Paid	Total Gain $	Total Gain %	Market Val	Edit
CBGIK	Trade	**31.90**	0.00	0.00%	$0.00	3	$17.00	$4,457.76	87.20%	$9,570.00	Edit
EEMIR	Trade	**22.50**	0.00	0.00%	$0.00	3	$17.60	$1,457.76	27.55%	$6,750.00	Edit
⊞ EWCIG	Trade	**4.80**	0.30	6.67%	$360.00	12	$4.30	$581.01	11.22%	$5,760.00	Edit
FTIJJ	Trade	**19.00**	8.00	72.73%	$4,000.00	5	$10.10	$4,436.26	87.61%	$9,500.00	Edit
IOKIZ	Trade	**30.50**	0.00	0.00%	$0.00	2	$30.00	$88.51	1.47%	$6,100.00	Edit
⊞ OBCAL	Trade	**16.00**	-0.50	-3.03%	-$200.00	4	$14.00	$787.01	14.02%	$6,400.00	Edit
OIIJJ	Trade	**27.60**	0.80	2.99%	$240.00	3	$16.60	$3,287.76	65.86%	$8,280.00	Edit
OJLAB	Trade	**7.50**	0.70	10.29%	$560.00	8	$7.00	$384.01	6.84%	$6,000.00	Edit
OLIAX	Trade	**10.20**	0.00	0.00%	$0.00	8	$7.65	$2,027.01	33.05%	$8,160.00	Edit
OMUAE	Trade	**13.30**	0.30	2.31%	$180.00	6	$11.70	$945.51	13.44%	$7,980.00	Edit
OPQAN	Trade	**29.80**	0.00	0.00%	$0.00	2	$29.80	-$11.49	-0.19%	$5,960.00	Edit
OYGAG	Trade	**41.00**	0.00	0.00%	$0.00	4	$20.40	$8,227.01	100.66%	$16,400.00	Edit
OYZAJ	Trade	**25.50**	2.00	8.51%	$600.00	3	$16.50	$2,687.76	54.16%	$7,650.00	Edit
TIEIG	Trade	**46.50**	2.20	4.97%	$1,100.00	5	$14.50	$15,986.26	220.08%	$23,250.00	Edit
TNBIH	Trade	**13.00**	0.00	0.00%	$0.00	5	$10.60	$1,186.26	22.32%	$6,500.00	Edit
UMUEF	Trade	**6.40**	0.20	3.23%	$200.00	10	$4.70	$1,687.51	35.81%	$6,400.00	Edit
UMUEG	Trade	**1.90**	0.25	15.15%	-$250.00	-10	$1.90	-$12.49	-0.65%	-$1,900.00	Edit
VHFAL	Trade	**23.80**	1.20	5.31%	$360.00	3	$21.40	$707.76	11.00%	$7,140.00	Edit
VOIAM	Trade	**27.20**	1.20	4.62%	$480.00	4	$20.70	$2,587.01	31.20%	$10,880.00	Edit

Symbol		Current Price	Change $	Change %	Day's Gain	Qty	Price Paid	Total Gain $	Total Gain %	Market Val	Edi
ZAMAJ	Trade	**5.80**	0.00	0.00%	$0.00	10	$5.40	$382.51	7.06%	$5,800.00	Edit
ZBKAF	Trade	**15.60**	1.30	9.09%	$520.00	4	$15.10	$187.01	3.09%	$6,240.00	Edit
ZSTAH	Trade	**11.90**	0.00	0.00%	$0.00	5	$9.80	$1,036.26	21.09%	$5,950.00	Edit
Cash						165.36				$165.36	
				Totals	$8,150.00		$121,831.39	$53,103.97	43.59%	$174,935.36	

LEGEND: ⊞ **collapsed** (click to expand) ⊟ **expanded** (click to collapse)

Real-time quotes

Portfolio Printer Friendly - Wachovia Securities, LLC

PORTFOLIO

Current date: Jan 15, 2006

Account Number:

Expand Detail Collapse Detail

▲ Description	Symbol	Quantity	Avg. Cost[1]	Price	Market Value	Unreal. Gain/(Loss) $[1]	Unreal. Gain/(Loss) %[1]
Stocks							
Common Stock							
ALLEGHENY TECHNOLOGIES	ATI	270.000	$36.35	$40.20	$10,854.00	$1,038.34	10.578%
AMERISOURCEBERGEN CORP	ABC	240.000	$41.55	$41.42	$9,940.80	($31.15)	(0.312%)
APPLE COMPUTER INC	AAPL	300.000	$64.83	$85.59	$25,677.00	$6,228.34	32.025%
BHP BILLITON LTD	BHP	250.000	$35.06	$35.84	$8,960.00	$196.05	2.237%
CAMECO CORP	CCJ	300.000	$57.48	$73.02	$21,906.00	$4,662.09	27.036%
GOOGLE INC CL A	GOOG	140.000	$371.25	$466.25	$65,275.00	$13,299.80	25.589%
INTERSTATE NET BK		3,500.000	N/A	N/A	N/A	N/A	N/A
RIO TINTO PLC	RTP	50.000	$183.82	$196.69	$9,834.50	$643.55	7.002%
SOWSTN ENERGY CO	SWN	200.000	$37.54	$40.70	$8,140.00	$632.06	8.419%
Total Stocks					**$160,587.30**	**$26,669.08**	
▲ Description	Symbol	Quantity	Avg. Cost[1]	Last Trade	Market Value	Unreal. Gain/(Loss) $[1]	Unreal. Gain/(Loss) %[1]
Options							
EXPRESS SCRIPTS INC CALL XTQ JAN 45 EXP 01/21/2006	XTQ-AI	9.000	$17.65	$42.80	$38,610.00	$22,728.78	143.117%
UNITEDHEALTH GROUP CALL UHB JAN 40 EXP 01/21/2006	UHB-AH	12.000	$16.70	$20.37	$25,080.00	$5,045.04	25.181%
Total Options					**$63,690.00**	**$27,773.82**	
Portfolio Total					**$224,277.30**	**$54,442.90**	

Prices are delayed at least 20 minutes.

[1]Securities with intra-day activity will not display information in the following data fields: Buy Date, Average Cost/Current Face Value, Total Cost, Unrealized Gain/Loss $, and Unrealized Gain/Loss % values. Securities with intra-day activity will also be displayed in italics.

PORTFOLIO

Current date: May 10, 2006 4:33 PM ET

Account Number:

Expand Detail Collapse Detail

▲ Description	Symbol	Quantity	Avg. Cost[1]	Price	Market Value	Unreal. Gain/(Loss) $[1]	Unreal. Gain/(Loss) %[1]
Cash/Cash Equivalents							
Deposit Cash Balance (IRA only)					$3.97		
Total Cash/Cash Equivalents					**$3.97**		
▲ Description	Symbol	Quantity	Avg. Cost[1]	Last Trade	Market Value	Unreal. Gain/(Loss) $[1]	Unreal. Gain/(Loss) %[1]
Options							
AKAMAI TECH INC CALL OMU JAN 25 EXP 01/20/2007	OMU-AE	1.000	$11.64	$12.72	$1,280.00	$115.75	9.942%
BHP BILLITON LTD CALL BHP MAY 25 EXP 05/20/2006	BHP-EE	2.000	$10.38	$24.10	$4,820.00	$2,744.50	132.233%
CAMECO CORP CALL ZBK JAN 25 EXP 01/20/2007	ZBK-AE	1.000	$14.34	$20.60	$2,010.00	$575.75	40.143%
FMC TECHNOLOGIES INC CALL FTI OCT 50 EXP 10/21/2006	FTI-JJ	1.000	$12.24	$20.90	$2,240.00	$1,015.75	82.969%
IPSCO INC CALL OPQ JAN 80 EXP 01/20/2007	OPQ-AP	1.000	$20.74	$32.57	$3,320.00	$1,245.75	60.058%
ISHARES MSCI CANADA CALL EWC SEP 21 EXP 09/16/2006	EWC-IG	2.000	$4.58	$4.80	$940.00	$24.00	2.620%
ISHARES MSCI EAFE INDEX CALL ZST JAN 60 EXP 01/20/2007	ZST-AH	1.000	$11.34	$11.90	$1,220.00	$85.75	7.560%
ISHARES TR MSCI EMERGING CALL EEM DEC 90 EXP 12/16/2006	EEM-LR	1.000	$20.64	$23.60	$2,360.00	$295.75	14.327%
MCDERMOTT INTL INC CALL OYZ JAN 50 EXP 01/20/2007	OYZ-AJ	1.000	$17.14	$25.90	$2,530.00	$815.75	47.586%
NVIDIA CORP CALL OLI JAN 22 1/2 EXP 01/20/2007	OLI-AX	2.000	$8.07	$9.12	$1,780.00	$165.76	10.269%
OCEANEERING INTL INC CALL OII OCT 60 EXP 10/21/2006	OII-JL	1.000	$15.14	$16.40	$1,750.00	$235.75	15.569%
PEABODY ENERGY CORP CALL BTU JUN 40 EXP 06/17/2006	BTU-FH	2.000	$10.37	$31.90	$6,400.00	$4,325.74	208.544%
TITANIUM METALS CORP NEW CALL TIE SEP 35 EXP 09/16/2006	TIE-IG	1.000	$16.44	$47.50	$5,490.00	$3,845.75	233.891%
TOYOTA MTR CORP ADR F CALL TM OCT 115 EXP 10/21/2006	TM-JC	1.000	$13.94	$12.40	$1,150.00	($244.25)	(17.518%)
TRANSOCEAN INC CALL VOI JAN 60 EXP 01/20/2007	VOI-AL	1.000	$22.94	$31.20	$3,120.00	$825.75	35.992%
Total Options					**$40,410.00**	**$16,073.25**	
Portfolio Total					**$40,413.97**	**$16,073.25**	

Portfolio Printer Friendly - Wachovia Securities, LLC

PORTFOLIO

Current date: Apr 18, 2006

Account Number:

Expand Detail Collapse Detail

▲ Description	Symbol	Quantity	Avg. Cost[1]	Price	Market Value	Unreal. Gain/(Loss) $[1]	Unreal. Gain/(Loss) %[1]
Cash/Cash Equivalents							
Money Market Fund					$4,290.99		
Brokerage Cash Balance					$385.73		
Total Cash/Cash Equivalents					**$4,676.72**		
▲ Description	Symbol	Quantity	Avg. Cost[1]	Price	Market Value	Unreal. Gain/(Loss) $[1]	Unreal. Gain/(Loss) %[1]
Stocks							
Common Stock							
ALLEGHENY TECHNOLOGIES	ATI	601.017	$38.89	$72.58	$43,621.81	$20,250.77	86.649%
AMERISOURCEBERGEN CORP	ABC	300.000	$45.75	$47.43	$14,229.00	$504.06	3.673%
CAMECO CORP	CCJ	800.358	$31.43	$41.54	$33,246.87	$8,091.89	32.168%
CB RICHARD ELLIS GROUP	CBG	200.000	$68.07	$84.31	$16,862.00	$3,247.04	23.849%
CIGNA CORPORATION	CI	100.000	$131.69	$125.76	$12,576.00	($592.95)	(4.503%)
E*TRADE FINANCIAL CORP	ET	900.000	$25.30	$26.00	$23,400.00	$627.13	2.754%
FRONTIER OIL CORP	FTO	200.000	$60.70	$61.88	$12,376.00	$235.04	1.936%
GOLDMAN SACHS GROUP INC	GS	100.000	$157.15	$164.96	$16,496.00	$781.05	4.970%
INVESTMENT TECHNOLOGY	ITG	500.000	$47.05	$53.99	$26,995.00	$3,470.16	14.751%
IPSCO INC	IPS	300.000	$93.54	$110.04	$33,012.00	$4,949.15	17.636%
LEHMAN BROTHERS HOLDINGS	LEH	100.000	$147.15	$154.26	$15,426.00	$711.05	4.832%
NVIDIA CORP	NVDA	600.000	$29.09	$28.93	$17,358.00	($96.72)	(0.554%)
THOMAS & BETTS CORP	TNB	300.000	$50.45	$52.28	$15,684.00	$549.06	3.628%
TITANIUM METALS CORP NEW	TIE	200.000	$49.82	$59.13	$11,826.00	$1,861.04	18.676%
TRANSOCEAN INC	RIG	200.000	$80.67	$85.25	$17,050.00	$916.11	5.678%
Total Stocks					**$310,158.69**	**$45,503.88**	

E*TRADE FINANCIAL

Open An Account | Help Center

QUOTES | SEARCH | LOG OFF

Accounts | Trading & Portfolios | Quotes & Research | Mutual Funds, ETFs & Bonds | Retirement & Advice | Banking & Credit Cards | Mortgages & Home Equity

Trade Portfolios View Orders | Balances | Transaction History | IPO Center | Account Records | Power E*TRADE

October 12, 2006 10:49 AM ET

Portfolios

Alerts | Transfer Money | Bill Pay | Help

Portfolios | Performance & Value | Positions | Gains & Losses | NEW: Risk Analyzer

Account/Watch List: LEGACY PUBLISHING LLC Create / Edit List **View:** Performance Customize / Reset

Market Value: $437,428.43 ($62,114.84 / 16.99%) **DJIA** 11,922.57 ▲ +70.44 **Nasdaq** 2,327.20 ▲ +18.93

REFRESH | STREAMING QUOTES | EXPORT TO EXCEL

Results per Page: 200

Symbol		Current Price	Change $	Change %	Day's Gain	Qty	Price Paid	Total Gain $	Total Gain %	Market Val	Edit
YVCAT	Trade	**162.30**	0.00	0.00%	$0.00	1	$146.00	$1,616.26	11.08%	$16,230.00	Edit
WTCAK	Trade	**144.50**	0.00	0.00%	$0.00	1	$129.50	$1,489.26	11.49%	$14,450.00	Edit
WSDAH	Trade	**51.00**	3.10	6.47%	$310.00	1	$47.40	$349.26	7.35%	$5,100.00	Edit
WJFAC	Trade	**41.90**	0.00	0.00%	$0.00	1	$40.50	$131.26	3.23%	$4,190.00	Edit
WLAAL	Trade	**28.30**	0.00	0.00%	$0.00	2	$25.10	$630.51	12.54%	$5,660.00	Edit
YMJAK	Trade	**22.60**	0.00	0.00%	$0.00	3	$21.20	$407.76	6.40%	$6,780.00	Edit
WAPAJ	Trade	**19.90**	0.00	0.00%	$0.00	3	$20.00	-$42.24	-0.70%	$5,970.00	Edit
WWDAL	Trade	**19.00**	0.00	0.00%	$0.00	3	$18.80	$47.76	0.84%	$5,700.00	Edit
⊞ WXUAJ	Trade	**18.40**	0.00	0.00%	$0.00	6	$18.00	$215.52	1.99%	$11,040.00	Edit
⊞ WJNAJ	Trade	**16.60**	0.00	0.00%	$0.00	6	$16.50	$37.52	0.38%	$9,960.00	Edit
WDFAF	Trade	**15.50**	0.00	0.00%	$0.00	3	$15.50	-$12.24	-0.26%	$4,650.00	Edit
YYOAJ	Trade	**15.40**	0.00	0.00%	$0.00	3	$15.40	-$12.24	-0.26%	$4,620.00	Edit
IYDLJ	Trade	**14.00**	0.00	0.00%	$0.00	2	$13.00	$190.51	7.30%	$2,800.00	Edit
WBAAH	Trade	**14.47**	0.00	0.00%	$0.00	4	$12.80	$657.01	12.80%	$5,788.00	Edit
WMRAF	Trade	**13.10**	0.00	0.00%	$0.00	4	$12.10	$389.01	8.02%	$5,240.00	Edit
WWRAE	Trade	**11.80**	0.00	0.00%	$0.00	4	$12.05	-$100.00	-2.07%	$4,720.00	Edit
WPGAK	Trade	**10.80**	0.00	0.00%	$0.00	5	$11.20	-$213.74	-3.81%	$5,400.00	Edit

Symbol		Current Price	Change $	Change %	Day's Gain	Qty	Price Paid	Total Gain $	Total Gain %	Market Val	Edi
⊞ WMNAF	Trade	**11.90**	0.00	0.00%	$0.00	10	$11.18	[illegible]	6.08%	$11,900.00	Edit
⊞ WPWAF	Trade	**11.00**	0.00	0.00%	$0.00	10	$10.75	$222.52	2.06%	$11,000.00	Edit
WMMAF	Trade	**10.10**	0.00	0.00%	$0.00	4	$10.40	-$130.99	-3.14%	$4,040.00	Edit
FXCB	Buy / Sell	**12.80**	0.00	0.00%	$0.00	14,000	$10.00	$39,200.00	28.00%	$179,200.00	Edit
ROMA	Buy / Sell	**15.03**	0.05	0.33%	$156.20	3,124	$10.00	$15,713.72	50.30%	$46,953.72	Edit
⊞ WJPAH	Trade	**10.00**	0.20	2.04%	$200.00	10	$9.75	$222.52	2.28%	$10,000.00	Edit
WFEAE	Trade	**8.70**	0.00	0.00%	$0.00	6	$8.20	$285.51	5.79%	$5,220.00	Edit
WLEAF	Trade	**7.90**	0.20	2.60%	$120.00	6	$8.10	-$134.49	-2.76%	$4,740.00	Edit
WDSAE	Trade	**8.30**	0.10	1.22%	$60.00	6	$8.00	$165.51	3.44%	$4,980.00	Edit
YTIAV	Trade	**7.90**	0.00	0.00%	$0.00	7	$7.60	$194.76	3.65%	$5,530.00	Edit
⊞ WGEAF	Trade	**7.60**	0.20	2.70%	$280.00	14	$7.30	$389.52	3.80%	$10,640.00	Edit
NFSAH	Trade	**7.50**	0.00	0.00%	$0.00	5	$6.80	$338.26	9.91%	$3,750.00	Edit
WMFAE	Trade	**5.00**	0.30	6.38%	$300.00	10	$4.90	$82.51	1.68%	$5,000.00	Edit
WPEAE	Trade	**4.10**	0.20	5.13%	$200.00	10	$4.70	-$617.49	-13.09%	$4,100.00	Edit
TTHBF	Trade	**3.80**	0.00	0.00%	$0.00	6	$2.30	$887.51	63.74%	$2,280.00	Edit
QQQVK	Trade	**0.05**	0.00	0.00%	$0.00	11	$1.10	-$1,171.24	-95.51%	$55.00	Edit
Cash						9,741.71				$9,741.71	
				Totals	$1,626.20		$365,571.88	$62,114.84	16.99%	$437,428.43	

LEGEND: ⊞ **collapsed** (click to expand) ⊟ **expanded** (click to collapse) Real-time quotes

SCHEDULE D (Form 1040)
Department of the Treasury
Internal Revenue Service (99)

Capital Gains and Losses

► Attach to Form 1040. ► See instructions for Schedule D (Form 1040).
► Use Schedule D-1 to list additional transactions for lines 1 and 8.

OMB No. 1545-0074
2004
Attachment Sequence No. **12**

Name(s) shown on Form 1040 | Your social security number

Part I Short-Term Capital Gains and Losses—Assets Held One Year or Less

(a) Description of property (Example: 100 sh. XYZ Co.)	(b) Date acquired (Mo., day, yr.)	(c) Date sold (Mo. day, yr.)	(d) Sales price (see the instructions)	(e) Cost or other basis (see the instructions)	(f) Gain or (loss) Subtract (e) from (d)
1 5 GGG Call Options	01/13/04	04/27/04	4,110	2,600	1,510
5 MKC Call Options	01/15/04	04/27/04	4,235	2,410	1,825
12 HCBK Call Options	10/20/03	04/01/04	37,302	16,448	20,854
800 Shs PBCT	01/30/04	03/05/04	36,008	30,094	5,914
1000 Shs NWSB	06/15/04	12/23/04	25,204	22,240	2,964
7 **Net short-term capital gain or (loss).** Combine lines 1 through 6 in column (f)				7	66,467

Part II Long-Term Capital Gains and Losses—Assets Held More Than One Year

(a) Description of property (Example: 100 sh. XYZ Co.)	(b) Date acquired (Mo., day, yr.)	(c) Date sold (Mo. day, yr.)	(d) Sales price (see the instructions)	(e) Cost or other basis (see the instructions)	(f) Gain or (loss) Subtract (e) from (d)
8 18099 Shs PFS	01/17/03	03/09/04	349,330	192,519	156,811
15 **Net long-term capital gain or (loss).** Combine lines 8 through 14 in column (f). Then go to Part III on the back.				15	159,042

KIA **For Paperwork Reduction Act Notice, see instructions.** **Schedule D (Form 1040) 2004**

Schedules A&B (Form 1040) 2004 OMB No. 1545-0074 Page **2**

Name(s) shown on Form 1040. Do not enter name and social security number if shown on other side. | Your social security number

Schedule B—Interest and Ordinary Dividends

Attachment Sequence No. **08**

Part I Interest

(See the instructions for Form 1040, line 8a.)

			Amount
1	List name of payer. If any interest is from a seller-financed mortgage and the buyer used the property as a personal residence, see instructions and list this interest first. Also, show that buyer's social security number and address ►		
	See attached worksheet(s) for detail.		9,089
4	Subtract line 3 from line 2. Enter the result here and on Form 1040, line 8a ►	4	9,089

Note: If line 4 is over $1,500, you must complete Part III.

Part II Ordinary Dividends

			Amount
5	List name of payer. ►		
	Wachovia # 0874		3,793
	Wachovia # 7184		9,483
	Wachovia # 6260		3,778
6	Add the amounts on line 5. Enter the total here and on Form 1040, line 9a ►	6	17,054

Buy Write Income Trade Confirmations

CUSIP: 125509JCC **Trade Date:** 08/31/05 **Settlement Date:** 09/01/05 **Transaction Number:** 000401825 **Market:** Chicago Board Options Exchange

Activity	Quantity	Security Description	Price	Principal
You Sold	2.000	CIGNA CORPORATION OCT (2005) 115 CALL **CI.JC**	4.20000	**$840.00**

Account Type: Margin

Commission	15.00
Regulatory Fee	0.04
NET AMOUNT	**$824.96**

ADDITIONAL INFORMATION OPENING TRANSACTION
As Agent for you we have sold or bought this security.

CUSIP: 01988PJWC **Trade Date:** 08/26/05 **Settlement Date:** 08/29/05 **Transaction Number:** 000270568 **Market:** Chicago Board Options Exchange

Activity	Quantity	Security Description	Price	Principal
You Sold	6.000	ALLSCRIPTS HEALTHCARE OCT (2005) 17 1/2 CALL **MXQJW**	1.20000	**$720.00**

Account Type: Margin

Commission	19.00
Regulatory Fee	0.04
NET AMOUNT	**$700.96**

ADDITIONAL INFORMATION OPENING TRANSACTION
As Agent for you we have sold or bought this security.

CUSIP: 09067DIRC **Trade Date:** 08/22/05 **Settlement Date:** 08/23/05 **Transaction Number:** 000110019 **Market:** Chicago Board Options Exchange

Activity	Quantity	Security Description	Price	Principal
You Sold	1.000	MERRILL LYNCH BIOTECH HOLDERS SEP (2005) 190 CALL **GBZIR**	4.20000	**$420.00**

Account Type: Margin

Commission	15.00
Regulatory Fee	0.02
NET AMOUNT	**$404.98**

ADDITIONAL INFORMATION OPENING TRANSACTION
As Agent for you we have sold or bought this security.

CUSIP: 88031MJEC **Trade Date:** 09/16/05 **Settlement Date:** 09/19/05 **Transaction Number:** 000897758 **Market:** Chicago Board Options Exchange

Activity	Quantity	Security Description	Price	Principal
You Sold	2.000	TENARIS SA-ADR OCT (2005) 125 CALL **TS.JE**	3.60000	**$720.00**

Account Type: Margin

Commission	15.00
Regulatory Fee	0.04
NET AMOUNT	**$704.96**

ADDITIONAL INFORMATION OPENING TRANSACTION
As Agent for you we have sold or bought this security.

CUSIP: 481165JJC **Trade Date:** 09/13/05 **Settlement Date:** 09/14/05 **Transaction Number:** 000753012 **Market:** Chicago Board Options Exchange

Activity	Quantity	Security Description	Price	Principal
You Sold	4.000	JOY GLOBAL INC OCT (2005) 50 CALL **JQYJJ**	1.90000	**$760.00**

Account Type: Margin

Commission	15.00
Regulatory Fee	0.04
NET AMOUNT	**$744.96**

ADDITIONAL INFORMATION OPENING TRANSACTION
As Agent for you we have sold or bought this security.

CUSIP: 345425VIP **Trade Date:** 09/27/05 **Settlement Date:** 09/28/05 **Transaction Number:** 000268082 **Market:** International Securities Exchange

Activity	Quantity	Security Description	Price	Principal
You Sold	4.000	FORDING CANADIAN COAL TRUST OCT (2005) 45	3.70000	**$1,480.00**
Account Type: Margin		**FDGVI**	Commission	15.00
			Regulatory Fee	0.07
			NET AMOUNT	**$1,464.93**

ADDITIONAL INFORMATION OPENING TRANSACTION
As Agent for you we have sold or bought this security.

CUSIP: 704549VQP **Trade Date:** 09/27/05 **Settlement Date:** 09/28/05 **Transaction Number:** 000270239 **Market:** Chicago Board Options Exchange

Activity	Quantity	Security Description	Price	Principal
You Sold	2.000	PEABODY ENERGY CORPORATION OCT (2005) 85	5.30000	**$1,060.00**
Account Type: Margin		**BTUVQ**	Commission	15.00
			Regulatory Fee	0.05
			NET AMOUNT	**$1,044.95**

ADDITIONAL INFORMATION OPENING TRANSACTION
As Agent for you we have sold or bought this security.

CUSIP: 91913YJCC **Trade Date:** 09/13/05 **Settlement Date:** 09/14/05 **Transaction Number:** 000770937 **Market:** Philadelphia Stock Exchange

Activity	Quantity	Security Description	Price	Principal
You Sold	1.000	VALERO ENERGY CORPORATION OCT (2005) 115 CALL	4.30000	**$430.00**
Account Type: Margin		**VLOJC**	Commission	15.00
			Regulatory Fee	0.02
			NET AMOUNT	**$414.98**

ADDITIONAL INFORMATION OPENING TRANSACTION
As Agent for you we have sold or bought this security.

CUSIP: 29250AJKC **Trade Date:** 09/19/05 **Settlement Date:** 09/20/05 **Transaction Number:** 000961556 **Market:** Chicago Board Options Exchange

Activity	Quantity	Security Description	Price	Principal
You Sold	3.000	ENCANA CORP OCT (2005) 55 CALL	1.85000	**$555.00**
Account Type: Margin		**ECAJK**	Commission	15.00
			Regulatory Fee	0.03
			NET AMOUNT	**$539.97**

ADDITIONAL INFORMATION OPENING TRANSACTION
As Agent for you we have sold or bought this security.

CUSIP: G5876HJWC **Trade Date:** 08/23/05 **Settlement Date:** 08/24/05 **Transaction Number:** 000155419 **Market:** Chicago Board Options Exchange

Activity	Quantity	Security Description	Price	Principal
You Sold	3.000	MARVEL TECHNOLOGY GROUP LTD OCT (2005) 47 1/2 CALL	1.85000	**$555.00**
Account Type: Margin		**UVMJW**	Commission	15.00
			Regulatory Fee	0.03
			NET AMOUNT	**$539.97**

ADDITIONAL INFORMATION OPENING TRANSACTION
As Agent for you we have sold or bought this security.

CUSIP: 01988PJWC **Trade Date:** 08/23/05 **Settlement Date:** 08/24/05 **Transaction Number:** 000156363 **Market:** Chicago Board Options Exchange

Activity	Quantity	Security Description	Price	Principal
You Sold	8.000	ALLSCRIPTS HEALTHCARE OCT (2005) 17 1/2 CALL	1.30000	**$1,040.00**
Account Type: Margin		**MXQJW**	Commission	22.00
			Regulatory Fee	0.05
			NET AMOUNT	**$1,017.95**

ADDITIONAL INFORMATION OPENING TRANSACTION
As Agent for you we have sold or bought this security.

CUSIP: 156782JQC **Trade Date:** 09/19/05 **Settlement Date:** 09/20/05 **Transaction Number:** 000964586 **Market:** Chicago Board Options Exchange

Activity	Quantity	Security Description	Price	Principal
You Sold	3.000	CERNER CORPORATION OCT (2005) 85 CALL	2.05000	**$615.00**
Account Type: Margin		**CQNJQ**	Commission	15.00
			Regulatory Fee	0.03
			NET AMOUNT	**$599.97**

CUSIP: 156782JQC	Trade Date: 09/14/05	Settlement Date: 09/15/05	Transaction Number: 000791449	Market: Chicago Board Options Exchange

Activity	Quantity	Security Description	Price	Principal
You Sold	2.000	CERNER CORPORATION OCT (2005) 85 CALL CQNJQ	3.20000	$640.00
Account Type: Margin			Commission	15.00
			Regulatory Fee	0.03
			NET AMOUNT	$624.97

SOLD CALL GOOGLE INC CL A $320 EXP 10/22/05			QUANTITY 1.00000	PRICE 7.90000	PRINCIPAL 790.00
SYMBOL	GGDJD	ACCOUNT TYPE	MARGIN	CHARGE/COMMISSION	11.25
SECURITY NUMBER	4289-174	TRADE DATE	09/20/05	OTHER FEE*	0.04
UNSOLICITED		SETTLEMENT DATE	09/21/05		
				NET AMOUNT	$778.71

*SEE ITEM 16 ON PAGE 2

MARKET AMERICAN STOCK EXCHANGE
TRADE INFORMATION: OPENING TRANSACTION.

SOLD CALL SUNCOR ENERGY $60 EXP 10/22/05 ****LONG TERM OPTION****			QUANTITY 2.00000	PRICE 2.90000	PRINCIPAL 580.00
SYMBOL	SUJL.	ACCOUNT TYPE	MARGIN	CHARGE/COMMISSION	12.50
SECURITY NUMBER	4278-477	TRADE DATE	09/16/05	OTHER FEE*	0.03
UNSOLICITED		SETTLEMENT DATE	09/19/05		
				NET AMOUNT	$567.47

*SEE ITEM 16 ON PAGE 2

MARKET CHICAGO BOARD OPTIONS EXCHANGE
TRADE INFORMATION: OPENING TRANSACTION.

SOLD CALL LONE STAR TECH INC $60 EXP 10/22/05			QUANTITY 2.00000	PRICE 2.20000	PRINCIPAL 440.00
SYMBOL	LSSJL	ACCOUNT TYPE	MARGIN	CHARGE/COMMISSION	12.50
SECURITY NUMBER	4475-397	TRADE DATE	09/16/05	OTHER FEE*	0.02
UNSOLICITED		SETTLEMENT DATE	09/19/05		
				NET AMOUNT	$427.48

*SEE ITEM 16 ON PAGE 2

MARKET PHILADELPHIA STOCK EXCHANGE
TRADE INFORMATION: OPENING TRANSACTION.

SOLD CALL NEXEN INC $50 EXP 10/22/05			QUANTITY 3.00000	PRICE 2.00000	PRINCIPAL 600.00
SYMBOL	NXYJJ	ACCOUNT TYPE	MARGIN	CHARGE/COMMISSION	13.75
SECURITY NUMBER	4537-241	TRADE DATE	09/16/05	OTHER FEE*	0.03
UNSOLICITED		SETTLEMENT DATE	09/19/05		
				NET AMOUNT	$586.22

*SEE ITEM 16 ON PAGE 2

MARKET CHICAGO BOARD OPTIONS EXCHANGE
TRADE INFORMATION: OPENING TRANSACTION.

SOLD CALL ALTRIA GROUP INC $75 EXP 10/22/05			QUANTITY 2.00000	PRICE 1.60000	PRINCIPAL 320.00
SYMBOL	MOJO.	ACCOUNT TYPE	MARGIN	CHARGE/COMMISSION	12.50
SECURITY NUMBER	4609-628	TRADE DATE	09/16/05	OTHER FEE*	0.02
UNSOLICITED		SETTLEMENT DATE	09/19/05		
				NET AMOUNT	$307.48

*SEE ITEM 16 ON PAGE 2

MARKET CHICAGO BOARD OPTIONS EXCHANGE
TRADE INFORMATION: OPENING TRANSACTION.

SOLD	QUANTITY	PRICE	PRINCIPAL
CALL ALTRIA GROUP INC $70 EXP 09/17/05	2.00000	2.80000	560.00

SYMBOL	MOIN.	ACCOUNT TYPE	MARGIN	CHARGE/COMMISSION	12.50
SECURITY NUMBER	4609-583	TRADE DATE	09/08/05	OTHER FEE*	0.03
UNSOLICITED		SETTLEMENT DATE	09/09/05		
				NET AMOUNT	**$547.47**

*SEE ITEM 16 ON PAGE 2

MARKET CHICAGO BOARD OPTIONS EXCHANGE
TRADE INFORMATION: OPENING TRANSACTION.

SOLD	QUANTITY	PRICE	PRINCIPAL
CALL ALLSCRIPTS HLTHCARE $17.50 EXP 09/17/05	5.00000	1.00000	500.00

SYMBOL	MXQIW	ACCOUNT TYPE	MARGIN	CHARGE/COMMISSION	28.75
SECURITY NUMBER	4526-885	TRADE DATE	09/07/05	REGULATORY FEE	0.03
UNSOLICITED		SETTLEMENT DATE	09/08/05		
				NET AMOUNT	**$471.22**

MARKET CHICAGO BOARD OPTIONS EXCHANGE
TRADE INFORMATION: OPENING TRANSACTION.

SOLD	QUANTITY	PRICE	PRINCIPAL
CALL WELLPOINT INC $75 EXP 09/17/05	4.00000	2.00000	800.00

SYMBOL	WLPIO	ACCOUNT TYPE	MARGIN	CHARGE/COMMISSION	27.00
SECURITY NUMBER	4593-816	TRADE DATE	09/07/05	REGULATORY FEE	0.04
UNSOLICITED		SETTLEMENT DATE	09/08/05		
				NET AMOUNT	**$772.96**

CONTINUED

SOLD	QUANTITY	PRICE	PRINCIPAL
CALL SUNCOR ENERGY $60 EXP 10/22/05 ****LONG TERM OPTION****	2.00000	2.75000	550.00

SYMBOL	SUJL.	ACCOUNT TYPE	MARGIN	CHARGE/COMMISSION	12.50
SECURITY NUMBER	4278-477	TRADE DATE	09/16/05	OTHER FEE*	0.03
UNSOLICITED		SETTLEMENT DATE	09/19/05		
				NET AMOUNT	**$537.47**

SOLD	QUANTITY	PRICE	PRINCIPAL
CALL MERIDIAN BIOSCIENCE $25 EXP 10/22/05	6.00000	1.60000	960.00

SYMBOL	ZUGJE	ACCOUNT TYPE	MARGIN	CHARGE/COMMISSION	30.50
SECURITY NUMBER	4965-058	TRADE DATE	08/23/05	REGULATORY FEE	0.05
UNSOLICITED		SETTLEMENT DATE	08/24/05		
				NET AMOUNT	**$929.45**

MARKET AMERICAN STOCK EXCHANGE
TRADE INFORMATION: OPENING TRANSACTION.

SOLD	QUANTITY	PRICE	PRINCIPAL
CALL CHESAPEAKE ENERGY $40 EXP 11/19/05	4.00000	1.25000	500.00

SYMBOL	CHKKH	ACCOUNT TYPE	MARGIN	CHARGE/COMMISSION	15.00
SECURITY NUMBER	4148-426	TRADE DATE	09/21/05	OTHER FEE*	0.03
UNSOLICITED		SETTLEMENT DATE	09/22/05		
				NET AMOUNT	**$484.97**

*SEE ITEM 16 ON PAGE 2

MARKET CHICAGO BOARD OPTIONS EXCHANGE
TRADE INFORMATION: OPENING TRANSACTION.

SOLD CALL NATIONAL-OILWELL $60 EXP 10/22/05

		QUANTITY 3.00000	PRICE 2.55000	PRINCIPAL 765.00
SYMBOL	NOVJL	ACCOUNT TYPE	MARGIN	CHARGE/COMMISSION	25.25
SECURITY NUMBER	4546-978	TRADE DATE	08/23/05	REGULATORY FEE	0.04
UNSOLICITED		SETTLEMENT DATE	08/24/05	**NET AMOUNT**	**$739.71**

CONTINUED

SOLD CALL VIROPHARMA INC $15 EXP 09/17/05

QUANTITY 5.00000 — PRICE 1.25000 — PRINCIPAL 625.00

SYMBOL	DUZIC	ACCOUNT TYPE	MARGIN	CHARGE/COMMISSION	28.75
SECURITY NUMBER	4185-043	TRADE DATE	08/30/05	REGULATORY FEE	0.03
UNSOLICITED		SETTLEMENT DATE	08/31/05	**NET AMOUNT**	**$596.22**

MARKET AMERICAN STOCK EXCHANGE
TRADE INFORMATION: OPENING TRANSACTION.

SOLD CALL FORDING CANDIAN COA $125 EXP 10/22/05

QUANTITY 3.00000 — PRICE 5.00000 — PRINCIPAL 1,500.00

SYMBOL	FDGJE	ACCOUNT TYPE	MARGIN	CHARGE/COMMISSION	25.25
SECURITY NUMBER	4243-802	TRADE DATE	08/30/05	REGULATORY FEE	0.07
UNSOLICITED		SETTLEMENT DATE	08/31/05	**NET AMOUNT**	**$1,474.68**

MARKET CHICAGO BOARD OPTIONS EXCHANGE
TRADE INFORMATION: OPENING TRANSACTION.

SOLD CALL TRANSOCEAN INC $55 EXP 09/17/05

QUANTITY 2.00000 — PRICE 3.00000 — PRINCIPAL 600.00

SYMBOL	RIGIK	ACCOUNT TYPE	MARGIN	CHARGE/COMMISSION	23.50
SECURITY NUMBER	4772-040	TRADE DATE	08/30/05	REGULATORY FEE	0.03
UNSOLICITED		SETTLEMENT DATE	08/31/05	**NET AMOUNT**	**$576.47**

MARKET CHICAGO BOARD OPTIONS EXCHANGE

SOLD CALL NEXEN INC $50 EXP 10/22/05

QUANTITY 3.00000 — PRICE 1.55000 — PRINCIPAL 465.00

SYMBOL	NXYJJ	ACCOUNT TYPE	MARGIN	CHARGE/COMMISSION	13.75
SECURITY NUMBER	4537-241	TRADE DATE	09/14/05	OTHER FEE*	0.02
UNSOLICITED		SETTLEMENT DATE	09/15/05	**NET AMOUNT**	**$451.23**

*SEE ITEM 16 ON PAGE 2

MARKET CHICAGO BOARD OPTIONS EXCHANGE
TRADE INFORMATION: OPENING TRANSACTION.

SOLD CALL NATIONAL-OILWELL $65 EXP 10/22/05

QUANTITY 2.00000 — PRICE 2.75000 — PRINCIPAL 550.00

SYMBOL	NOVJM	ACCOUNT TYPE	MARGIN	CHARGE/COMMISSION	12.50
SECURITY NUMBER	4547-011	TRADE DATE	09/14/05	OTHER FEE*	0.03
UNSOLICITED		SETTLEMENT DATE	09/15/05	**NET AMOUNT**	**$537.47**

*SEE ITEM 16 ON PAGE 2

MARKET CHICAGO BOARD OPTIONS EXCHANGE
TRADE INFORMATION: OPENING TRANSACTION.

SOLD				QUANTITY	PRICE	PRINCIPAL
CALL NATIONAL-OILWELL				2.00000	2.55000	510.00
$60 EXP 10/22/05						
SYMBOL	NOVJL	ACCOUNT TYPE	MARGIN		CHARGE/COMMISSION	23.50
SECURITY NUMBER	4546-978	TRADE DATE	08/26/05		REGULATORY FEE	0.03
UNSOLICITED		SETTLEMENT DATE	08/29/05			
					NET AMOUNT	**$486.47**

MARKET CHICAGO BOARD OPTIONS EXCHANGE
TRADE INFORMATION: OPENING TRANSACTION.

SOLD				QUANTITY	PRICE	PRINCIPAL
CALL MERIDIAN BIOSCIENCE				4.00000	1.50000	600.00
$25 EXP 10/22/05						
SYMBOL	ZUGJE	ACCOUNT TYPE	MARGIN		CHARGE/COMMISSION	27.00
SECURITY NUMBER	4965-058	TRADE DATE	08/26/05		REGULATORY FEE	0.03
UNSOLICITED		SETTLEMENT DATE	08/29/05			
					NET AMOUNT	**$572.97**

CONTINUED

SOLD				QUANTITY	PRICE	PRINCIPAL
CALL FLORIDA ROCK IND				3.00000	1.65000	495.00
$60 EXP 10/22/05						
SYMBOL	FRKJL	ACCOUNT TYPE	CASH		CHARGE/COMMISSION*	19.75
SECURITY NUMBER	4276-322	TRADE DATE	09/26/05		OTHER FEE**	0.03
UNSOLICITED		SETTLEMENT DATE	09/27/05			
					NET AMOUNT	**$475.22**

*INCLUDES $6.00 TRANSACTION FEE
**SEE ITEM 16 ON PAGE 2

MARKET CHICAGO BOARD OPTIONS EXCHANGE
TRADE INFORMATION: OPENING TRANSACTION.

SOLD				QUANTITY	PRICE	PRINCIPAL
CALL FLORIDA ROCK IND				3.00000	1.70000	510.00
$60 EXP 10/22/05						
SYMBOL	FRKJL	ACCOUNT TYPE	CASH		CHARGE/COMMISSION	13.75
SECURITY NUMBER	4276-322	TRADE DATE	09/26/05		OTHER FEE*	0.03
UNSOLICITED		SETTLEMENT DATE	09/27/05			
					NET AMOUNT	**$496.22**

*SEE ITEM 16 ON PAGE 2

MARKET CHICAGO BOARD OPTIONS EXCHANGE
TRADE INFORMATION: OPENING TRANSACTION.

SOLD				QUANTITY	PRICE	PRINCIPAL
CALL FLORIDA ROCK IND				3.00000	1.85000	555.00
$60 EXP 10/22/05						
SYMBOL	FRKJL	ACCOUNT TYPE	CASH		CHARGE/COMMISSION	13.75
SECURITY NUMBER	4276-322	TRADE DATE	09/26/05		OTHER FEE*	0.03
UNSOLICITED		SETTLEMENT DATE	09/27/05			
					NET AMOUNT	**$541.22**

*SEE ITEM 16 ON PAGE 2

MARKET CHICAGO BOARD OPTIONS EXCHANGE
TRADE INFORMATION: OPENING TRANSACTION.

SOLD
CALL FORDING CANDIAN COA
$125 EXP 09/17/05

QUANTITY 1.00000 | PRICE 5.50000 | PRINCIPAL 550.00

SYMBOL	FDGIE	ACCOUNT TYPE	MARGIN	CHARGE/COMMISSION	11.25
SECURITY NUMBER	4243-800	TRADE DATE	09/09/05	OTHER FEE*	0.03
UNSOLICITED		SETTLEMENT DATE	09/12/05		
				NET AMOUNT	**$538.72**

*SEE ITEM 16 ON PAGE 2

MARKET CHICAGO BOARD OPTIONS EXCHANGE
TRADE INFORMATION: OPENING TRANSACTION.

SOLD
CALL EDISON INTL
$45 EXP 09/17/05

QUANTITY 5.00000 | PRICE 1.20000 | PRINCIPAL 600.00

SYMBOL	EIXII	ACCOUNT TYPE	MARGIN	CHARGE/COMMISSION	28.75
SECURITY NUMBER	4221-730	TRADE DATE	09/06/05	REGULATORY FEE	0.03
UNSOLICITED		SETTLEMENT DATE	09/07/05		
				NET AMOUNT	**$571.22**

MARKET INTERNATIONAL SECURITIES EXCHANGE
TRADE INFORMATION: OPENING TRANSACTION.

SOLD
CALL VIROPHARMA INC
$15 EXP 10/22/05

QUANTITY 10.00000 | PRICE 1.85000 | PRINCIPAL 1,850.00

SYMBOL	DUZJC	ACCOUNT TYPE	MARGIN	CHARGE/COMMISSION	37.50
SECURITY NUMBER	4185-018	TRADE DATE	08/23/05	REGULATORY FEE	0.08
UNSOLICITED		SETTLEMENT DATE	08/24/05		
				NET AMOUNT	**$1,812.42**

MARKET INTERNATIONAL SECURITIES EXCHANGE
TRADE INFORMATION: OPENING TRANSACTION.

SOLD
CALL CHESAPEAKE ENERGY
$40 EXP 10/22/05

QUANTITY 8.00000 | PRICE 0.95000 | PRINCIPAL 760.00

SYMBOL	CHKJH	ACCOUNT TYPE	MARGIN	CHARGE/COMMISSION	20.00
SECURITY NUMBER	4148-484	TRADE DATE	09/28/05	OTHER FEE*	0.04
UNSOLICITED		SETTLEMENT DATE	09/29/05		
				NET AMOUNT	**$739.96**

*SEE ITEM 16 ON PAGE 2

MARKET CHICAGO BOARD OPTIONS EXCHANGE
TRADE INFORMATION: OPENING TRANSACTION.

SOLD
CALL TENARIS S A SPONSOR
$110 EXP 09/17/05

QUANTITY 2.00000 | PRICE 2.50000 | PRINCIPAL 500.00

SYMBOL	TSIB.	ACCOUNT TYPE	MARGIN	CHARGE/COMMISSION	23.50
SECURITY NUMBER	4780-928	TRADE DATE	08/29/05	REGULATORY FEE	0.03
UNSOLICITED		SETTLEMENT DATE	08/30/05		
				NET AMOUNT	**$476.47**

MARKET CHICAGO BOARD OPTIONS EXCHANGE
TRADE INFORMATION: OPENING TRANSACTION.